THINKING OUT LOUD

Fresh Perspectives on Daily Life

By

Carol L. MacAllister

ISBN 0-7414-2801-6

ABOUT THE COVER: The cover is an original painting by the author who is also a folk artist. Inquiries about her work and for a CD of her paintings, contact the author at carolmacallister@pobox.com .

Published by:

INFI∞ITY
PUBLISHING.COM

1094 New DeHaven Street, Suite 100
West Conshohocken, PA 19428-2713
Info@buybooksontheweb.com
www.buybooksontheweb.com
Toll-free (877) BUY BOOK
Local Phone (610) 941-9999
Fax (610) 941-9959

Printed in the United States of America

Printed on Recycled Paper

Published September 2005

TABLE OF CONTENTS

§

ACKNOWLEDGMENTS

I wish to thank Steve Klinger, publisher and editor of *The Las Cruces Bulletin* in the 1980's and early 90's. He gave me a chance, despite his newspaperman's instincts, to offer my perspective on life. *The Las Cruces Bulletin* is now owned and published by David E. and Jacqueline McCollum. They have given their blessing to this project.

I also want to thank my dear friend and colleague, Diane Coker, whose steadfast support and unflinching honesty helped me stay true to what I wanted to say when first writing my column.

Dru Sharp, my typist with the patience of a saint, read as she typed and wouldn't let me change too much. And special thanks go to Esther Roush, Mary Simmons and Cindy Murrell for their critical and essential editing.

§

INTRODUCTION

This book is a compilation of the newspaper columns I wrote for our local weekly newspaper, *The Las Cruces Bulletin*. They are best read one or two pieces at a time. I arranged them according to the season of the year in which they were originally published. Some of them are season specific, but most are what I was thinking of or talking to others about at that time of year.

I began my column in 1984. At first the editor rejected my idea for a personal reflection column on the basis that it was not really newspaper fare. But I persisted and he took a chance.

The demands of my personal and professional life forced me to discontinue my column in 1985. In the following years, friends would request different columns for themselves as they struggled with a particular issue or problem. Others told me that they had saved certain columns that touched them and re-read them from time to time. Always they asked me when I would write again.

I resumed my column in August 1993 and began compiling this book shortly thereafter. Now, a decade later, here are the original columns with minor editing to bring the writing into present-day lexicon and political/cultural sensibilities.

I hope reading my thoughts will do for you what writing them has done for me: entertain, teach, comfort and even inspire.

CLM, 2005   Las Cruces, NM

SPRING

§

If Love Is So Great, What Is Going Wrong?

I thought of writing this for the Valentine's Day edition of the paper but, after all, one hates to be a royal stick-in-the-mud intentionally, not to speak of hurting the local candy and flower businesses. Nevertheless, one can't help but be struck by the juxtaposition of the folderol of Valentine's Day with the reality of the most recent national statistics on marriage. Nearly 50 percent of all marriages end in divorce.

If love is so great, what is going wrong?

Sociological and psychological theories are many. Toffler's *Future Shock* (published in 1970), is no longer the future; it is here. The depressed economy and the realities of unemployment have crushed personal dreams. It is hard to dream and see the world as wonderful when all bets could be called off in an instant. The trouble with these explanations is that they are so global, so beyond the individual's power to change today...here...now.

Let me suggest a closer-to-home explanation. It is what I call a preventive idea, not an after-the-fact cure. Namely, that *falling* in love as a reason for marriage is for the birds. Birds can at least spread their wings and glide before hitting the ground when they have soared to dizzying heights.

The American Heritage Dictionary defines *to fall* as "to drop without restraint, to be severely wounded or to be killed in battle; to collapse from lack of structural support, to strike bottom." No matter how you slice it, to fall is not to rise.

Why not walk into love instead? I can hear the groans of protest now. The whole point to falling in love is to get that rush, that quickening of your pulse when the object of your desires comes near. A tried and true friend who has been around for years seeing you through thick and thin can't do that for you.

This new fellow or gal makes you swoon. Your old friend just makes you feel comfortable, even a little bored at times. But when you get through swooning, will your new heartthrob like you when you are at your meanest, bluest or ugliest?

Your old friend must, because he has already seen you like that and he is still around. And what is a marriage partner but someone who will be your friend in foul weather as well as fair? To have a friend as a mate is really something to swoon over.

The trouble is such people are rarely dashing, beautiful or irresistibly sexy. They are just folks with such often invisible qualities as loyalty, generosity, patience, endurance, and reliability. There is nothing very exciting here, just comfort, like a good pair of walking shoes. Not pretty or fashionable, but durable and good for the long haul.

Do you have such a friend in your life? Stop and look at him or her again.

What I am suggesting is that walking into love is a far superior way to approaching relationships, especially those you are considering for a lifetime.

Walking is slow going, however. It takes one step at a time and you don't get anywhere fast. There is no soaring to great heights, no being swept off your feet by wine and roses.

Yes, you can get hurt even when you walk into love, but your odds are better. You aren't going as fast or as high as when you fall in love, so at the worst you will be bruised, not brokenhearted.

Even if you are so foolish as to *fall* in love, the bloom does come off the rose. No one can live at the mountaintop all the time. The air is too thin. Why don't you and your love consider walking down here in the valley with the rest of us not-so-exciting mortals? You just might avoid becoming a national statistic before the honeymoon is over?

§

The Fickle Finger of Accusation

Criticism, a noun meaning to "censure, reprove, reproach, disapprove, condemn," is found everywhere. Whether over the backyard fence, at the office or in the church foyer, it seems to be the human condition to find fault in others.

Similarly, haven't you noticed how captivating bad news is? When is there more good news than bad on the TV? In spite of our public protests to the opposite, we lend a willing ear to the latest gossip. For many, the news is an addiction even with its continuous recounting of one massacre or earthquake or flood or accident after another.

Why? Why are we attracted to bad news when common sense would dictate the opposite? Why do we willingly participate in gossip that would cut us to the quick if we were the subject of such degrading whispers?

Movies are another venue of negativity and angst. The idea of attending a horror film makes me cringe. Life is scary enough, and yet hundreds of thousands pay good money to be scared out of their wits. The theory, of course, is that to be a little scared is exciting.

Movies are pretend. They are not really happening to us. Gossip and bad news about others are not *our* realities either. Perhaps that is why they are so perversely mesmerizing. As we watch others' misfortunes, we privately whisper, "There but for the grace of God go I," and thus feel better about our own lots in life.

I think criticism is much the same. To find fault in others serves to inversely buoy us up. We are better than the one we are pointing an accusatory finger at. We *know* we don't make such stupid mistakes in judgment, or perform as poorly on the job.

But stop. What is this? Look at your hand. Yes, that's right, the one with the index finger pointing out toward the one you are criticizing. Take a good look. What do you see? There are three fingers pointing back at you. Oh, they may be curled up a little in a fist, but there is no mistaking it. They are pointing directly back at you.

Think about the criticism you are launching at the other person. Is it not your greatest weakness, too, or the inverse of your own failings? For example, there is the husband who criticizes his wife's emotionalism when in fact his own emotional repertoire is sadly impoverished. And what about the *A* student called an egghead by the *C* student who doubts his own innate intelligence.

Daily criticism and gossip are only the little sisters to the big brother called prejudice. To prejudge another is to decide who and what a person is before he has had the opportunity to present himself. We hate it when it is done to us, but are often too eager to do it to others.

I think of prejudice as two men standing in a pond of quicksand. One is standing on the shoulders of the other; the one on top thinks he is superior. Both are sinking. Both are doomed; one just goes down before the other. And so it is with this whole family of finding fault in others. The envy revealed from prejudice, gossip and criticism serves only to deflect attention from yourself and all that you are failing to do, could do better, and could become.

§

No Place to Roar

I was never a *Hillstreet Blues* fan for the simple reason that I prefer the investigative journalism of programs like *20/20* and *Nightline*. However, one Thursday night I did watch a re-run of *Hillstreet Blues* so I could see the pilot program that put the popular television series on its award-winning path. It was well done and captivating, in spite of the apparent mayhem of a big city police precinct.

However, as engrossing as the intertwining stories were, the thing that interested me the most was the emotionality that I guessed was the real reason for the series' popularity. After all, there is a plethora of shoot 'em up stories on television and the question to ask is "why?" Why so many and why so popular? What basic human emotion is expressed or appealed to that keeps the audience coming back for more? What is the magnetism of violence?

Having not watched the program before, I was not conditioned to the chaos of the police headquarters or to the intense and often loud confrontations between colleagues. I was even more surprised to find out at the end of the program that the captain and the lawyer, who had fiery encounters in the beginning of the hour were, in fact, lovers.

The thing about all this that fascinates me is the tolerance for, the expectation of, and the acceptance of so much interpersonal violence and confrontation. In this program (and so many like it) people always seem to be shouting at each other rather than talking.

The police issues are intermingled with personal sagas of broken marriages, alcoholism, nervous breakdowns and new loves. There is no separation of personal versus professional issues, no proper time or place for husbands and wives to iron out their differences, no rules of propriety whatsoever.

And yet, when one person loses control of himself, another seems to keep his cool, thus offering a counter-balance that keeps the chaos just barely under control. That may be the base line I am looking for here. Controlled violence: controlled explosions of human emotion that allow the frustrations and tension of this intense kind of job to be vented as a safety valve would on a steam engine.

This American society of ours does not make much room for strong emotions, be they sorrow and grief, joy and exuberance, or anger to the point of explosion. From the stoic New Englander, to the macho cowboy, to the cool executive, to the soothing unflappable secretary, we are a nation which rewards, respects and reveres a cool, calm and collected demeanor.

To lose control of one's emotions is to shame one's self, to lose face. But not to express one's emotions from time to time is to invite heart attacks, ulcers and nervous breakdowns.

So what have we done to help ourselves out? We have institutionalized the expression of violent or very strong emotions. The big business of professional football is an excellent example. As in *Hillstreet Blues*, the players execute physical violence against each other within certain rules, allowing enough control to prevent really serious injury while permitting some good thrashings. The crowd roars its approval, screaming to its favorite gladiators to "kill" the enemy.

Television also offers this vicarious expression of powerful emotions through the many police/detective type programs. The actors shout at each other and say all the things we wish we could say to the people in our lives that frustrate us. They hit people who assault them, often taking justice into their own hands. All are things we wish we could do from time to time as well.

I, for one, am forever biting my tongue as I check my impulse to speak in anger to someone who no doubt deserves a good tongue lashing. Just listen to the violence in those popular phrases. I've often wished I could yell at my lover or best friend in the morning and know that it would be forgotten that evening, that it was all just a part of the day's business.

I wish I could be as tolerant of all the pathology (unusual behaviors) that seems to be so acceptable to those folks on *Hillstreet Blues*.

A fifty-year-old sergeant dating a seventeen-year-old high school student and a street detective who likes to bite ankles are unusual to me. Yet the tolerance of such types on this program was strangely comforting. So there it is. Television programs like *Hillstreet Blues* give us a place to roar our own unspoken rages and idiosyncrasies without even opening our mouths or risking our secret selves.

The trouble is vicarious living doesn't really seem to work. If it did, wouldn't we have our fill of such programs instead of needing more? Addictions, after all, become just that because they only treat the symptom and not the cause.

Vicarious expression of aggressive feelings strikes me as safe in the short run and dangerous in the long run. For it is not the same as the real thing. Where do you find a place to roar?

§

What You See Is What You Get

Since it is spring, it is naturally a time for beginnings. It is no wonder that spring is the most popular time of year for love to blossom into marriage proposals and wedding bells to fill the air in June. With the incidence of divorce bordering on fifty percent, I can't help but wonder what sage advice all those divorcees would give to all those newlyweds, given the chance.

Not being a member of either group, I will stand apart and with the perspective of an armchair quarterback, offer this advice to all embarking on a relationship of any significance.

"What you see is what you get."

This may seem like a harsh and most certainly a shallow point of view, but there is more here than meets the eye. In fact, the eye is the key. Are you really seeing what is right in front of you? I never cease to be amazed at how blind those with perfectly good eyes can be. I guess our selective seeing has more to do with what we want to see or need to see, than it does with what is really out there.

Even when we do see obvious differences, we neatly rationalize them by saying opposites attract. This provides the argument for counterbalances and beneficial influences. All can lead to disaster a few years down the marital trail, unless you scout out the terrain very carefully and make sure that what begins as a small pebble in your shoe does not become the Rock of Gibraltar as you travel along.

Perhaps the person you want to befriend or even marry is, and has been all his or her life, a pleasant, flexible and laid-back person. If you are a firebrand who has little tolerance and less patience, then at first glance your laid-back guy may look like just the counterbalance you need. Over time, however, he will not become more like you nor you like him. Rather, you will become an ever sharper thorn in his soft side and he will seem more like a dead weight dragging at your heels.

How about the helpless little maid who needs her manly man at every turn, which makes him feel powerful and protective? This works fine until he can't depend on her to do a thing for herself, or even take command should he need to relinquish the helm for a rest or for good.

An easier place to see what I am getting at here is to take a look at how people handle illness, large or small. For ten years I was a social work consultant to kidney dialysis, leukemia and burn patients. I can tell you that how a patient was before he became ill or injured is how he was after he became a patient.

Optimistic souls who have always taken each day and each problem in stride do the same with their illness. Those who have always viewed themselves as victims of life no matter how favorable their lives may be, become more dependent, more demanding and more complaining than ever.

They say that as we grow older, we don't change, we just become more so. I agree with that and I would say that the principle holds true "in sickness and in health."

Opposites do attract, but they do not wear well over time, for we all become more so as we age. Ignorance is only bliss in the movies where the script can be easily changed. Take a good look at the person you want to love and cherish for the rest of your life and then look again. Is what you see what you want for the long haul? Really?

§

Spring Cleaning

I spent this past couple of weekends going through a ritual that seems peculiar to springtime and is almost perversely gratifying...spring cleaning.

I say perversely gratifying because for fifty weeks out of the year, I, and I think most of us, spend our time and resources accumulating things in the firm conviction that more is better, a motto that could probably be printed on American dollar bills.

Then, in two short weeks, I seem to become crazed with the need to throw away boxes and boxes of old and not-so-old clothes; magazines I swore one day I would read; bits and strips of cloth, string and leather saved for those someday craft projects; old purses; single mittens and gloves; straw hats that have too many holes to block the sun but hold so many memories.

There were books with passages that once seemed to be written just for me; cans of odd screws and nails I will probably want the minute they are gone; rubber bands from the newspapers thrown on the lawn.

Also included was a roll of butcher paper I'll want the next time I move; empty boxes saved for Christmas and then forgotten; half cans of paint and stiff paint brushes, and a dozen yardsticks gathered during my annual treks to state and county fairs.

The list went on and on, and as the pile of things to be got rid of grew larger, my sense of elation and freedom expanded proportionately.

When I finally collapsed at the end of the day, my exhaustion was the kind that comes when you know you have done something good for yourself.

"But how strange," I thought, "that throwing things out could make me feel so good?" What is this business of purging the junk out of one's life? Is spring cleaning nothing more than the behavioral end of the same continuum as confession or screaming at a rock concert?

When you confess your secret sins, presumably you are cleansing your soul of the burden of guilt from "wrong" behavior. And when you go to a rock concert or to a football game you are permitted, even encouraged, to scream yourself hoarse, venting any and all pent-up rages and frustrations from your day-to-day life.

Then along comes spring cleaning, and you are once again offered your annual chance to cleanse your life of the objects d' growth that have lost their meaning or usefulness.

Spring cleaning is a reckoning with some hard truths. How many times are you going to repack that "thin" wardrobe for the day when you finally lose those extra ten pounds you have been carrying around for the past five years? When do you admit you are who and what you are and probably always will be?

When do you throw out those half cans of paint and turpentine, finally admitting to yourself that you are never going to repaint that old bookcase in the den or that old kitchen chair that doubles as a footstool?

When are you going to let go of the dream of setting up a corner workshop in the garage with every tool in its place and every nail and screw sorted by size and placed in the appropriate baby food jar?

When are you going to stop saving scraps of cloth for that rag rug you were going to braid for the sun porch?

When are you going to stop stockpiling for all those projects you want to do when you finally have some free time? There is no such thing as free time!

Springtime is not only a time of new love and newly-weds, it is also a time of letting go and cleaning house, literally and symbolically.

It would be interesting to know how many divorces or broken relationships occur in the spring and compare that data to how many marriages and new relationships are spawned. When do most people take on new jobs? When are the most houses sold? Cars traded in? Must there be a cleansing, a purging of the old before the new can be accommodated?

I've been refusing to buy any more food lately, until I use up all the cans of food, dry staples, and frozen food that have been on my shelves and in my refrigerator for many months. I'm enjoying the sense of creativity and resourcefulness it takes to devise a menu from seemingly so little.

It is surprising that so little turns out to be quite sufficient. I haven't spent a penny on groceries in a month, but I haven't lost a pound of flesh either! After living with the absolute conviction that *more is better* all these years, the idea that *less could be best* is positively exhilarating.

For more than forty years I have been a red-blooded American who knew exactly what to do whenever I felt a slump or depression coming on. When the going got tough, I went shopping.

My closets and cupboards have always been the picture of abundance and prosperity. But suddenly this year, and more so this year than in any previous year, the spring cleaning fever has hit me and I am cleaning out corners in my life I haven't looked at in years. Like I said, the pain of it is perversely pleasurable.

There is a sense of victory over an ancient and never-really-seen enemy. Is it a mid-life crisis or am I finally in touch with the rhythms of the earth that have always been there whispering in my ear? "Come follow me," the earth seems to say. "Unburden yourself, so that you might grow. Watch me and I will show you how."

§

Risking Enthusiasm

A *Passion for Excellence* was the title of a program on PBS given by Tom Peters, one of the co-authors of the best seller *In Search of Excellence*. The authors had intended to go out into the American business world, armed with scientific surveys, to discover the organizational structures that seemed to be the foundation of the most successful companies in America. What they actually found was not at all what they were expecting.

What Tom Peters found in the big-moneyed world of corporate America was that the most successful companies were so, not because of some fancy structure, but because the top man cared about the bottom-most man in his organization.

Furthermore, Peters found that the really effective leaders spent as little time as possible in their authority-laden corner offices, and were out among their employees and facilities serving as "cheerleaders, enthusiasts, nurturers, coaches and facilitators."

That is a novel way to define a leader, for most of us are accustomed to viewing a leader as someone who carries his authority well, who stands apart from the masses, and who, above all else, is the cool, calm and collected center of each storm that blows in.

An "enthusiastic cheerleader" does not fit that mold. Peters even quoted some elderly business tycoon as saying, "The older I get the more respect I have for enthusiasm."

I liked hearing that!

I am one who does everything with intensity, and my enthusiasm for life is often hard to keep under control. I am forever apologizing for my energy and excitement, as if I can't be considered a serious person unless I look serious, sound serious and above all act serious.

Over the years this problem of my enthusiasm has gotten worse because I am so delighted with my life. I'm effective at my job; my artistic endeavors are flourishing; I love writing; and I am surrounded by great friends. Every morning I go to work, I feel so happy that I want to hug everyone in sight, but I control myself, and just say the cheeriest "hello" I can muster.

Leo Buscaglia told us, shouted at us, and even scolded us to hug each other more often, but it is easier said than done. Some people don't like to be touched, let alone hugged, and such behavior is often considered suspect in the stately halls of the workplace.

Tom Peters sounded just like Leo Buscaglia the other night. He, too, shouted his message and scolded the audience for not daring to risk innovation and for fearing they'd be called "wacky" when they wanted to do something fun and different at work.

The more he scolded, the more the audience applauded. And therein is an interesting human dynamic: vicarious living. Neither Buscaglia nor Peters are telling us anything we don't already know.

The bottom line for both is to risk getting involved with others, and yet, we buy their books instead. We flock to their lectures and tune them in on television as if we might magically, vicariously, absorb the skills and secrets of relating successfully to others.

Listening to Peters, I was reminded of all the cookbooks I own although I rarely cook, and of all the investment books I've bought, yet still have never risked a penny. I wonder how many people just read these cookbooks of success but don't ever try the recipes?

Are you a gourmet cook if you subscribe to *Gourmet* magazine, or are you a gourmet cook if you go to the kitchen and make a mess trying new concoctions even without a cookbook?

I think I'll risk a few hugs tomorrow.

§

Ode to One's Bald Spots

In the February 1991 issue of *Parade Magazine*, Ted Danson revealed that he no longer wore the toupee that his *Cheers* character, Sam Malone, wore to keep up his sexual-lion image. It seems Ted is no longer afraid to show his bald spot.

Would it were so for us gals!

How I wish I could go without my make-up, which hides the pits and scars of an acne-plagued adolescence.

How I wish I could forgo the proper attire for the occasion, be it office, date or afternoon movie, and just wear what feels good.

How I wish I could forsake those uncomfortable, but oh, so fashionable shoes, and let my feet spread to their natural if ungainly width.

I've made some headway on the shoe front. Having canvassed every shoe store in the area to no avail, I ordered from Bass Co. in Maine a pair of web-sided shoes that actually looked stylish and were comfortable. Added to this positively rebellious attitude toward pointed-toed footwear, I also wear my Rockport walking shoes to and from work and on my lunch hour. So there!

And when I don't want to shave my legs, I wear slacks. Sometimes I wear slacks every day. My hair has been cut in a style that is for my convenience and lifestyle and no longer in the style favored by my man. Sorry, honey.

My all-time favorite photo is one of me happily collapsed after a hike wearing my khaki hat with the brim flipped up like Gabby Hayes and my old, hole-speckled sweater. It is ME and shows my "bald spots."

The hat was the one I wore daily as a National Park Ranger instead of the traditional regulation Smoky Bear version. That floppy ole hat went along while I fought a fire, went on a scary overnight rescue, led nature hikes, cleaned privies, and was even my main weapon in running off a porcupine. It's an old friend.

The sweater survived high school, a year in Europe, two trips across the country and several soakings on various wild river-rafting adventures.

The shoes have stretched to accommodate all the vagrancies of my inglorious feet and even the indestructible Vibran soles have been worn smooth. The ski parka was christened at Arapahoe Basin during my 1960's college days at the University of Colorado in Boulder. It doesn't fit anymore, or rather I don't fit it, but I have kept it for all the memories it evokes.

The outfit is a composite of my life and what I like to do best. It protects and warms me on each long and satisfying hike in the nearby Organ Mountains. Tired and happy, I am not caring a whit about my appearance, my posture, my poise or my clothes. It is a photo in which, like Ted Danson, I show my "bald spots." I wish I was brave enough to do so daily.

§

The Call of the Wild

I once had three dogs; actually two were mine and one was a boarder for a short while. The yellow Labrador, Sirius, was the quintessence of tolerance and patient good humor. The female Doberman, Sagebrush, was sweet and loving, but slow to warm up to a new person or dog in the household.

Taller but lighter than the male Lab, she demanded from him endless hours of play, and he complied until he tired, and then with one snap, the pecking order was restored.

Enter Lobo, a male Norwegian Elkhound whose even temperament seemed to contradict his fierce-sounding name.

His black and white face mask made him appear to have his eyebrows arched upward and his mouth in a perpetual smile. His playfulness gave the Doberman a run for her money and, after some initial testing, the trio lived and romped together quite nicely, though adding a third dog, however temporarily, seemed to quadruple the activity in the house.

Lobo, which means wolf, was found by a friend of mine in the desert near an ancient petroglyph site in the middle of New Mexico. He was only a few months old, starving and covered with fleas.

Lobo responded to the new care and love from my friend in leaps and bounds. He grew quickly and became as affectionate as any dog owner could hope. But my friend lived in the country where there were no fences and lots of temptation to roam, and roam Lobo did.

Whether it was a part of his breed or whether his early months of abandonment made him that way, Lobo could not be persuaded to stay close to home, especially when all humans had deserted him for their work-a-day worlds.

Eventually his wandering became a habit and a fortune was spent in newspaper ads, new collars and tags, and animal shelter fees. Threatened with a court appearance and stiff fine, my friend had to find a solution, and my big backyard with its eight-foot fence seemed ideal. They were not.

Each day Lobo scaled that eight-foot fence and found a sympathetic neighbor to take him in. An electric wire was strung around the top of the fence. That didn't stop him either. He found a loose board at the base of the fence, pulled it forward with his paw and slipped through.

Lobo's determination to be free and his need to be with other animals and humans struck a responsive chord in me. Whether it was due to his genetic instincts or to his early and forced independence, Lobo, like so many of us, seemed to be struggling with both his need for freedom and his need to belong.

The call of the wild begged him to make extraordinary efforts to gain his freedom, but the ever-present dog catcher or well-intentioned neighbor returned him to various hearths, which Lobo always seemed glad to see. He needed people and he needed to be away from people.

I often feel the same. Some mornings while driving to work, the temptation to keep going challenges my willpower and sense of responsibility. I often feel fenced in and wish I could find that hole in my "fences" just like Lobo had.

This tension between freedom and belonging also troubles me when I attend the circus. During intermission there are usually elephant rides for young and old alike. To be sure, I have climbed aboard, all the time feeling repulsed by the servitude of this magnificent beast.

My repulsion grows deeper as I watch the tigers, lions and leopards go through their unnatural paces or when the camel and llama trot around the ring in their pathetic tutus.

Perhaps we are repeating our own evolutionary domestication when we capture wild animals and try to humanize them.

Certainly my backpacking forays into the Gila Wilderness give me a sense of freedom and self-sufficiency that I can't experience any other way. I know people who need a wilderness "fix" every weekend or they are impossible to live with. Are they responding to an ancient call of the wild, remembered only in some recessive gene left over from a nomadic ancestor?

I admired Lobo's tenacious resourcefulness. The holes in the fence were plugged, the electric fence charged, and Lobo stayed with me without further escape. But in deference to his call of the wild, and perhaps in deference to mine, I took all three dogs to the desert every morning at sunrise to run free and untethered for a half hour, while I walked and dreamed of my wilder and freer days, epochs ago.

§

Moving West...Decisions from the Future

As I prepared to move from upstate New York, where I had been a psychiatric social worker, to a state some weren't sure was really in the Union and where I knew not a soul, had no job and no place to live, my friends asked WHY. After all, didn't I have everything?

I had a good job, maybe even the best of its kind in the area. I had colleagues I could share with and rely on for help when the going got rough. I had a large circle of warm and supportive friends, and I had my family all around.

Why then, would a single, young woman with everything going for her professionally and personally, strike out for such a place, desolate of friends, any guaranteed job, vegetation or sophistication? In short, how could anyone go from New York to New Mexico? I could. I did.

The first question is why? The second question is how? Not how did I actually travel west, but how did I make my decision.

To move west was not a new thing. Young men and women had been doing it for years, seeking a new life, a better and perhaps a fuller life in terms of testing themselves.

I was a very late comer to a long line of truly brave pioneers. After all, they traveled on foot and in wagons, without much hope of ever visiting home again. They went in spite of fears of death around every bend in the trail, with starvation and disease as constant companions, and with primitive living conditions even when they reached their destinations.

By contrast, my venture west is almost embarrassing to relate. I drove west in a BMW 2002 which worked perfectly the entire way. I had money in the bank and in my pocket. I slept in motels, dined in lovely restaurants, and enjoyed the pleasantries of an erudite traveling companion, who bested my adventure by returning east by bicycling alone all the way back to New York City.

In terms of pioneering, it added up to a very little splash after all. Nevertheless, I had given up a great deal, and the reason, I reckon, was that my life had become too comfortable.

I needed to stretch myself. I needed to see what I was made of, to see if I could make a life for myself away from the well-trod paths of my parents and their parents before them. I wanted to find not so much a better life, but a better me.

When my clients and friends asked me, "Why, but why?" I replied, "Because I want to become a very interesting old lady. If I stay in one place all my life, I'll never reach that goal."

When I became scared about leaving so much and so many loved ones behind, and when I began to wonder if New Mexico was as wild and woolly as everyone was saying, then I would think of that interesting old lady I wanted to become and say to myself, "When she is on her death bed looking back down the road of her life, knowing what she knows about life by then, will she be proud or ashamed of the decisions and moves she made as a younger woman?"

When I have tough decisions to make, I think of that interesting old lady I want to become and I conjure up her wisdom and ask, "If I could know today what she will know when she is 80, what would be her advice about this move?"

On my wall, hung just so I can read it each morning upon waking, I have a letter written by Nadine Stair of Louisville, Kentucky, when she was 85 years old. Of all its wisdom-embroidered lines, the ones I resonate to the most are, "If I had my life to live over, I would be sillier than I have been this trip. I would take fewer things seriously. I would eat more ice cream and fewer beans. I would perhaps have more actual troubles, but I'd have fewer imaginary ones."

Just before I moved west, I read a book titled *How People Change* by psychoanalyst Allen Wheelis. He wrote of discipline, willpower, and courage to push against the old, set and comfortable patterns we establish for security. His words touched me and I wrote to thank him. He actually wrote me back, and the interesting old lady of my old age to come cheered as I loaded the car and headed west.

§

If He's Mr. Right, Where Are the Bells?

Once upon a time there was a young woman, a Princess if you will, who met her Prince Charming and fell madly in love. Ah, the excitement of it all. The mention of his name would send her pulse racing. His face would make her heart pound wildly, and the touch of his hand on her arm nearly caused her to swoon.

When she was with him, she glowed in the warm protection of his strength and superior (of course) power. With him she would be safe for all time. With him she would feel like a queen. With him she would live happily ever after.

Then it happened. One day it seems, a former girlfriend of our Prince came to town and called him. Though she had treated him badly and had spurned him cruelly only the year before, the old spell was still there. He ran to her side, canceling without hesitation an important and long-standing date with our Princess. CRASH! When the Princess recovered, albeit tiara askew, she vowed never to choose a man with her heart again. She would use her head and be sensible.

The trouble is, when you let your head choose your romantic companions, the bells don't ring, the fireworks don't go off and your pulse stays more or less the same.

No wild and glamorous skiing holiday where you were stranded on a ski lift and forced to huddle while the cold north wind spun its icy arms of torrid romance around you. Is that a picture of an oxymoron?

No shipboard rendezvous on the high seas with stolen embraces in the moonlight at the stern of the ship. (By the way, have you ever really stood at the stern of a ship? Noisy!) No sireee. Not much romantic intrigue for you here and no bells!

What to do about it?

Then a friend, lamenting about the slam-bam-thank-you-ma'am climate in sex these days, wonders aloud, "Whatever became of the long kiss?"

Indeed, whatever became of taking your time, of holding hands, of linking arms while you walk? Whatever happened to long walks for that matter? Whatever happened to porch swings and sitting in silence listening to the night?

We are in such a hurry these days that we want our food while we wait in the car; we want our clothes cleaned in one day, if not one hour; we want our travel to be on the fastest jets; and we want to have a rich and intimate love relationship after the first date.

No wonder so many marriages end in divorce court and so many people end up on a shrink's couch. At the very least you are headed for indigestion, physically and emotionally.

Choosing a mate with your head is a good idea. So what if he isn't the handsomest man you've ever dated. So what if he isn't the most exciting and adventurous man you've hitched your star to. So what if he doesn't set you on fire with a single glance. You probably don't do all that for him, either.

When you use your head to find a partner for the long term, you will probably have mutual friends and common interests. Your approach to life will probably be similar and your sensitivities won't offend each other.

So what's the hurry? In time the bells may well ring, and if they do it will be a song of mutual respect and affection and the kind of love that will last a lifetime. When you meet Mr. or Miss Right from your head's point of view and the bells don't ring, stop and listen more carefully. Some silences are golden.

§

A Case for Good Manners

After an evening class at the university the other day, a group of us adjourned to a local bar for a convivial drink and conversation. One of my classmates is British, or so I surmised from her wonderfully proper accent, and I had been dying to know more about her for weeks.

Finally, I had the chance to get acquainted and in characteristic style for me, and for most Americans, I asked where she was from and how she happened to end up in Las Cruces. With characteristic British reserve and brevity, she answered, "London. My husband is from here and now works here."

Then I asked her that inevitable question, "What do you think of Americans?"

After some initial evasion she answered, "Americans ask a lot of personal questions, which in Europe is considered inappropriate and rude. We believe you can learn much more by being silent and observing than by asking questions. After all, a person will really tell you what they want you to know in time, don't you think?"

If you will read the above again, remembering to use a crisp British accent, you will know immediately that I had been put in my place. My natural curiosity and American friendliness was urging me to ask her even more questions, but now I was painfully self-conscious about my apparent bad manners.

Of course, I was not being rude by American standards, but by British standards I was, and once again I was reminded of how confident we Americans are about doing everything *our* way and how rarely we stop to consider that a totally different interpretation can be made of our behavior.

Let me give you another example.

As coordinator of a community education program, I met with several Moslem men from the Middle East who wanted to teach some classes for me.

Again, in characteristically American style, I stood up to greet them at the door of my office, hand extended in what I thought was a universal gesture of friendliness and good intention. The first man took my hand but very tentatively. The second not only would not take my hand, but backed out of the doorway. I pursued him and he backed up even farther. Finally, he told me, "I do not shake the hand of the woman."

This man then went on to explain that in conservative or orthodox Islamic cultures, men are not permitted to touch any women except their mothers, sisters, wives or daughters. He also seemed very reluctant to look me straight in the face, but denied that working for a woman would be difficult, a question I asked point-blank.

Since in many Islamic cultures men and women are segregated socially, he did prefer that his class be all male, but when in Rome....

I did assure him that he did not have to touch any of the women in his class, but that he did have to allow women to take the class.

Here again, I was confronted with how differently good manners are interpreted around the world. As offended as I was that this man would not take my hand, he was equally offended that I wanted him to do something that was totally against his religious beliefs and cultural customs.

All this has given me pause to consider the case of good manners even among my own friendly, nosey, handshaking kind.

While I rarely hesitate to remind an errant child to say "thank you" and "please," I too often forget to say those precious words myself. How little it takes to let others know that you appreciate even the smallest gestures or favors. And the situation gets worse the longer you know someone.

As familiarity takes over, we all become complacent and take each other for granted, forgetting how sweet those two little words of "please" and "thank you" can be.

They say familiarity breeds contempt, but it doesn't have to. The sharp edges of your life can be rounded off and made smooth by that ole-time elixir, "remember your manners."

However, in remembering your manners, you must also remember that what are acceptable manners to you may not be acceptable to someone else.

Probably, "thank you" and "please" are acceptable anywhere, but then, that is what I believed about the handshake and asking questions to show friendliness and interest.

It must be true that the road to misunderstanding-hell is paved with good intentions. My British classmate was right. Good intentions are not enough. One must learn to stop, look and listen.

§

Diamonds in the Rough

"There aren't any good men left. All the good ones are married!" Such are the laments heard weekly in half-whispered conversations over the Friday afternoon drink on the eve of yet another lonely weekend for the single females of this nation.

There is a book on the market that says the above is not true and tells the female lonely hearts how to remedy their dilemmas. The book is titled *Smart Women, Foolish Choices* and is about women who keep choosing the wrong men, why, and what to do about it.

The basic premise of the book is twofold. First is that men and women look for different things from relationships. Women are raised expecting to find excitement, fulfillment, even their identities in the men they love and marry. Men, on the other hand, are raised to expect excitement and fulfillment in their work, so they look to relationships with women to provide nurturance and security.

In looking for excitement, the woman is vulnerable to the charmer with the strong opening act and the accouterments to match. The trouble is the first act is the entire play with this kind of guy. There is no more.

Within a month the truth starts to come out. He doesn't call when he says he will and he forgets a few dates which he can always explain with some plausible, if not entirely believable, excuse. Keeping your hold on this guy is like holding on to water: no substance, and a guaranteed trail of tears.

The second premise of the book is that smart women are missing the obvious. The remedy, according to the authors, is to see this pretty fellow for what he isn't and go purposely, intelligently hunting for the "diamond in the rough."

The trouble is he is hard to see because he doesn't sparkle, at least not right away. This unpolished soul will probably fumble his way through the first date, and most assuredly not know one vintage wine from another. His car will not be the slick powerhouse that snaps your neck at each light, but it will get you home in one piece. Not knowing how to get the first kiss, he'll offer his hand and hit you in the stomach. Flashy he isn't, but dependable he is.

When you are in trouble, he'll come, and when you need a shoulder to cry on, his are broad enough to hold you even if they are not muscled and tanned.

I have gone into some detail here, for while this book, *Smart Women, Foolish Choices,* is written *by* men *for* women, I think men could get just as much out of it.

I, for one, am getting sick and tired of the seemingly endless stream of literature written *for* the woman to help her find her perfect mate or live happily without him: *The*

Cinderella Complex, How to Make Love to a Man, and *Why do I Feel Incomplete without a Man*?

Since when is it the woman's responsibility to remedy the interpersonal blues? Are there not men who choose the wrong women repeatedly? Are there not men who have guilt complexes, poor self-images and misguided expectations of their dream women?

Surely there are as many female "diamonds in the rough" awaiting some smart man who can go beyond fashion, beauty and sex appeal to see her core strengths for what they are and could offer him. Men too, are well-advised to look twice at the woman they call friend, but never considered a lover before. If it is nurturance men want most, who better to nurture him than a friend?

And lest you married folks feel left out of this discourse, look up from your reading and look at your mate. Has the complacency of time tarnished the sparkle of the gem you married? No doubt.

Who among us, young, old, single or married, does not wish to be more appreciated for all those qualities that make each of us unique? Who among us has not some rough edges we would like others to look beyond? I think this idea to go looking for "diamonds in the rough" is a dandy, but I don't think it is only the single female who needs to go mining.

§

Are Bad Habits Really Good Friends?

Everyone has a bad habit or two, or three, or more. Some are more apparently harmful than others, but all are irritating and targets for criticism from others.

Bad habits are also remarkably resistant to any and all manner of corrective measures from good old willpower to shock treatments. The question then is, "How come?" Is it possible that our bad habits really serve a useful purpose in our lives? Could it be that in our ordinary level of consciousness we want to be rid of them, but on a deeper level we work to preserve them?

Let's take one of the most stubborn of bad habits, smoking. Its evils in terms of lung cancer and social rejection these days are familiar to all of us. Just for the hell of it, let's turn the coin over and ask the impossible, or apparently impossible, question. How or why could smoking be good for you?

Let me share with you the example of a friend who, in questioning her own smoking habit, discovered how it was helping her maintain a deeply ingrained value.

My friend is a slender, crisp stereotype image of her British birthright. Even when she is relaxing, she has an all-business, no-nonsense air about her. Pragmatic and industrious, she likes to get the job and all jobs done well, completely, and on time. Idleness, thy name is not Diane.

In trying to discover why she really smoked, Diane began at the beginning and observed when she smoked, the most, the least. She discovered that she smoked the most when she sat down to relax and took a break from her busy schedule, and when she was at play, i.e. at a social gathering.

In other words, she realized, she smoked the most when she was not working and keeping busy. She smoked the most when she was goofing off, instead of doing something useful and productive. She smoked the least when she climbed into bed with a cup of hot tea and a book at the end of a good day's work. These times could not be considered goofing off because you are supposed to stop working when you go to bed. It is the legitimate time and place not to be busy and productive.

Next, she observed that when she did smoke the most, the smoking seemed to keep her hands very busy. She was always lighting, inhaling, tending the ashes, or waving the smoking wand in the air as she talked. Her hands were never idle as long as she had a cigarette in one of them.

Noticing this fundamental pattern in her life, that she needs to be busy to feel good, she asked herself what she believed about being busy and about busy people in general. Then she asked how that belief differed from what she thought about not being busy or about people who seem to do less than she. Ah hah!

To be busy, efficient, using every waking moment productively was good. To goof off or to be idle, accomplishing less than optimally possible was bad.

Her smoking then kept her busy even when she allowed herself to be idle. Her smoking habit was not an old behavior that was just hanging on for no reason, but was an active and important partner in maintaining her values about productivity.

When Diane then asked the next logical question, "Why wasn't being idle from time to time okay?" she could not produce a good answer. Could it be that relaxing and goofing off from time to time *was* okay? She did not have to be busy every minute of the day. So startling was this revelation that it just stopped her in her tracks. All she could do was sit down and not have a cigarette! She no longer smokes.

I used to smoke but gave it up when I finished four years of psychotherapy. Talking, and really communicating with others, had become a more satisfactory form of oral gratification than sucking on a tobacco lollipop.

But I still eat more than I need, usually when idly watching television. Eating keeps me very busy while supposedly goofing off! Well, what do you know?

Perhaps one of the reasons Diane and I are friends is because we are birds of a feather. In writing to you about her insights, I just stubbed my toe on one of my own most frustrating bad habits, eating when I am not hungry.

I, too, give no quarter to laziness in myself or in others. My belief in the value of productivity is so deep that my bad habit of eating while relaxing is really a *friend* who supports that belief. Idle hands need not do the devil's work. Move over, Protestant work ethic, here comes **nothing!**

§

As a Man Thinketh in His Heart

I was once asked to judge an Optimist Club speech contest. The topic all contestants had to address was *Think the Best, Expect the Best.*

Though the approach to the topic varied with each contestant, the fundamental message was the same and seemed to reflect the philosophy of the Optimist fraternity and could have been borrowed from the Scriptures, "As a man thinketh in his heart, so is he." (Proverbs, 23:7).

I don't think anyone would argue with this idea, but its simplicity disguises its profundity. That simple statement says that what you think *in your heart* about life, yourself and others can, in fact, create your realities. Think about that for a few minutes. It is really a powerful concept. Your thoughts, your inner thoughts from the heart, can create your reality.

It is important here to remember that there is often a big difference between what you think in your head and profess publicly, and what you think in your heart, in the most private recesses of your soul.

You don't always believe what you consciously say you believe. This is why it is not always easy to determine just exactly what it is you do believe or think deep in your heart.

Many of our inner beliefs are disguised or sub-conscious, and we often express these in more subtle ways such as through nonverbal behavior. Fingers half covering the mouth, arms folded across the chest, legs crossed or uncrossed, are readily recognized body language with meaning and hidden messages from deep within, usually without the sender's awareness.

Most of us have not developed our eye for such communication and therefore miss the real message being sent. This wouldn't be so bad if we were not also losing our ability to really listen to others and hear what they are saying.

Western man may be the telecommunications expert of the world, but he is a lousy listener. As a result, we can be in touch with the world, yet not in touch with ourselves or those we wish most to communicate with.

So how do you learn to listen? Really listen? The answer is to listen to what is being said. Listen to the *literal* meaning of the words.

Since most of us have fairly broad vocabularies, it is reasonable to assume that the words and phrases each of us apparently chooses to use have significance for us and therefore can be taken seriously and literally.

For example: If the proliferation of million dollar lotteries and sweepstakes is to be believed, everyone, it seems, would like to be rich. Yet most are not. Why?

If, "as a man thinketh in his heart, so is he," then let's listen literally to one man as he speaks of money and see if we cannot discover why he is not rich or richer...or is even poor.

"Man, that guy is filthy rich. Never had to work a day in his life! Lucky bastard! It should be against the law to have so much money without working for it."

The American dream is the rags to riches story. The self-made millionaire is the ultimate rugged individualist. Few begrudge him his success. But inheriting money is not the same thing. If you didn't earn it, maybe you think in your heart you don't really deserve it.

The guy who sees the rich as "filthy rich" sees money as unclean in some way, and that those who have not really earned their money are really "bastards," albeit lucky ones. If you don't sweat for every penny, you really don't deserve it, not legally.

The speaker of the above quotes tells us a great deal of his real, heart-deep beliefs about money. He is a hard working man who earns every penny, and because he believes money should not come too easily, it never comes too easily to him either.

He resents this reality and yet, "as a man thinketh in his heart...." If he were to be given a lot of money, he would probably spend it all. Easy come, easy go. Being a "bastard," lucky or not, does not suit him. And money you don't earn is illegitimate, against the law or ought to be. That's what he said. I heard him, didn't you? He could only speak of money and rich people differently if he believed differently. He says what he believes and "as a man thinketh in his heart, so is he."

This is only one example of how one person's beliefs held deep in his heart, as revealed in his language, literally help explain his realities, even when he thinks consciously something quite different. Your realities are a reflection of your beliefs. Stop and listen. Your heart is talking.

§

Making a Case for Mystery

Working on a college campus gives one ample opportunity to observe the dress of the inhabitants. I'm always amazed at men, young and old, who wear really tight pants, usually blue jeans. It is true cowboy fashion.

Presumably, the point to having their genitalia bulging out at the crotch is to attract women, and surely it works in the short run. I always look, don't you?

But I never (or rarely) look a second time. What for? The mystery is gone. Give me a man with boxer shorts and baggy pants, the kind Kevin Costner wears. Now there is a mystery worth pursuing.

Some blue jeans I've seen were so tight that the fabric over the bulge was worn white and appeared to even be threadbare. How does that happen, I wonder? Really gentlemen...is this the male's answer to the braless days of the 1960s?

And another thing about tight pants: they raise the temperature of the testicles, which kills the sperm. How ironic: the sexier a man may try to appear, the more impotent he may render himself.

There is an opposite case to the tight pants which I should mention. It is those very baggy slacks, mostly worn by middle-aged men, now adopted by high-schoolers that they are forever hitching up or otherwise adjusting. Whatever the reason for such chronic pulling and tugging, attention is drawn to that area at the very least. Guys—stop it! We can look all by ourselves, thank you. No directions needed.

Then there are those gold chains! Call me old-fashioned, call me conservative, call me unimaginative, but I think gold necklaces look better on women. I know men like to dress up, and some may feel they need to embellish what they have. And, of course, we do have nature's own example of the male of the species having all the color, size, hairy mane, antler rack, or roar in order to impress and corral the usually colorless, drab female of his choice. That's fine for the animal kingdom, but I don't care for decorated human males.

Somewhere along the evolutionary line, the human species got the decorating of oneself switched around so that it is the female who does the preening and primping to attract the male.

The only decor I want to see on a man's chest is his own indigenous hair and that is all I need. My imagination can do the rest. Once again, it is the mystery of discovery that I like. The mystery of not knowing everything right away, up front, so to speak; the mystery that gives my imagination a chance to exercise itself is much more interesting.

In a society where all forms of mass media tell all, share all and bare all, I'd like to make a case for the subtle titillation of mystery.

§

The Crisp New Woman

I'm worried about something. No actually, I'm worried about someone, someones, women! The women who grew up in the 50's and 60's saw the rebirth of women's liberation and have tried in varying degrees to cross over and become the *New Woman*.

They are the ones who have paid the highest price for the women's movement, for they are the ones who marched for abortion and against unequal pay. They are the ones who lectured, cajoled and stonewalled their men into seeing them as persons and not just as sex objects. They are the ones who filed the first women's discrimination suits, either individually or in a class action to demonstrate that they meant business.

I call these women who paved the way this time around for women's rights the transitional women, for they made the transition possible. They are the transition because they live in two worlds. While their heads tell them one thing, their instincts, their reflexes from their childhood training tell them another.

This struggle between the past and the present has resulted in some overreactions in an attempt to compensate for what is carelessly dubbed "typical female behavior." One area this is most evident is in the development of sharp edges in women's mannerisms and speech.

The very successful women I know, mostly professionals, academics, administrators, and business women, no longer smile spontaneously or allow themselves to get excited when they see a person they like. Their faces are studies of professional control in order, I assume, not to show any of that stereotypic feminine emotionalism men like to target to avert attention from their own emotional limitations.

These women stand and sit with a ramrod posture that is meant to portray power and strength but just looks uncomfortable to me. Their voices are crisp. The intonation is matter-of-fact and very businesslike. In fact, one could go so far as to call it abrupt. I always feel intimidated and irritated by this kind of rapid-fire speech. It chops each word in half and cuts me off before I have said all I intended.

Sharp edges do cut, and maybe that is what is needed at the top when there is only one woman in a pack of men who don't really want you there in the first place.

The transitional woman in a man's world must prove herself first, before any credit or assumption of competence is made by her male contemporaries. But surely she can be a strong woman without being so tough that even other women don't want to spend much time talking to her.

Yes, I know the sharp cutting speech and manners work when she wants to execute her business with efficiency. But I wish there were some way of turning it off, or applying it selectively so that I am not cut off and cut up by that crisp manner as well. I'm not the business at hand to be dealt with swiftly. I am a friend and want to be treated as such.

Perhaps I should be more understanding of these sisters of mine and remember all they have had to go through to get where they are. Success has a price, and when you are a transitional woman, it is higher, for it takes practice to be successful and fully yourself at the same time.

Women haven't had much time to practice. On top of that they have had to compensate for, and even hide, their femininity in order to have a chance at being treated as equals with men.

I can't imagine wanting to be like a man. I just want to be given equal opportunities and equal pay. I want to start with the same assumptions that my male peers get. Men are assumed competent until proven incompetent. Women are assumed incompetent, stupid and ignorant until they prove several times over that they are as good as any man, which by then means they are better than most. I resent having to act like a man to be given any semblance of equal treatment.

But I worry even more that to gain equal treatment; women will forsake their womanliness to make it in a man's world. I look forward to the day when we can be feminine and still be strong and powerful, even respected and admired as such.

When that day comes, perhaps we can speak once again in the flowing, melodious speech that *is* woman and still deliver the message. When that day comes, we will feel comfortable again with the spontaneous warmth that has for the history of mankind nurtured babies, tamed the beast in man, and civilized countless societies and frontiers.

§

I Have Met the Enemy and He Is Me

One of the best things I ever did as a teacher of young social work students was to assign them the task of being handicapped for twenty-four hours. They were to assume a handicap of their choice, provided it made them dependent on others. Never before had these young people, fully endowed with their health, brains and resources intact, had to depend so heavily and critically on the goodwill and actions of others.

Those who chose to be in a wheelchair were stunned that perfectly healthy and strong individuals seemed unable to hold a door open for them. These students felt a new indignation at the inaccessibility of many buildings to the handicapped and took seriously the federal regulations that required public buildings to be ramped for those who cannot traverse steps.

Some students chose to be speechless for the day. Most could not use sign language, but even those who could found a world that could not sign back. At first this handicap seemed easy enough. One could always take pad and pencil and write whatever one needed. However, writing is a slow process and the communicating of more than the simplest of needs was cumbersome and was met with impatience.

Soon, these students found themselves painfully isolated, unable to participate in the banter of their peers, or in class discussions, and unable to tell the teacher that their silence was not impertinence.

One student, who had chosen to be voiceless, had a flat tire on the way to school. How to call for help? With much embarrassment and shame, she admitted that she cheated on her assignment, calling her father for assistance, but the lesson of her helplessness, had she really been mute, was not lost.

All the students felt the isolation their handicap imposed on them and were incensed that people would not look them in the eyes, but averted their heads as if to deny this less-than-whole human being was really there.

They felt alone in the world, unable to relate to their peers as normal. Ignored or treated with irritation and impatience, they felt helpless. Even those who tried to be helpful did so in a condescending and degrading manner.

The handicap was more than just the inability to walk or talk or see. The students were treated as if they were also stupid and infantile. The mute student found people shouting at her as if she were deaf too.

The "blind" students wanted to scream at those who spoke in simple childlike sentences as if their blindness had prevented them from learning the complexities of the English language.

The "mute" student wanted to cry when her peers, even knowing this was an experiment, gave up talking to her except for the most perfunctory of yes or no questions. No one, it seemed, had the time it takes to walk with, talk with and be with a handicapped person.

I have a friend who was paralyzed from the upper chest down by a freak auto accident. In the space of six short months she returned home to where she resumed living independently with her teenage daughter, worked as a counselor, and got on with the business of life and learning to cope with her new limitations.

For this redoubtable lady, to go from being a free spirit who traveled and met adventure with total ease to being dependent on her many friends for even the simplest of needs was an adjustment that defied description. So, unfortunately, was the adjustment to the insensitivities of the people and agencies who were supposed to be the experts in rehabilitating those with disabilities!

Eventually, my friend bought a van and, after much delay, the local rehabilitation agency converted it so she could drive. The trouble was the job was done incorrectly and incompletely. The driver's seat was ten inches higher than the wheelchair.

Since my friend had to transfer from one to the other on a board, pulling herself up those ten inches was impossible. I couldn't do it, even with my fully functional back and chest muscles.

When she pointed this out to the rehab counselor, she was told, "You'll work it out." Work what out? Paralyzed muscles don't work out anything! Similarly, the conversion of the van left out switching the foot emergency brake to a hand controlled brake. Since when does putting a car in park sufficiently assure that it will not jump out of gear?

Seat belts bolted to the floor for the wheelchair were missing, as was a holding device to prevent the empty wheel chair from flying through the windshield or flying backward out of reach should a sudden stop be needed.

I used to have a fantasy of becoming the head of rehabilitation for the state. Before anyone took a job in my organization, I would require them to do what I had my social work students do. I would make them assume a handicap for a week, so they too could experience the helplessness, rage and frustration that is what being handicapped is so often about.

The argument against this in-kind experience is that you don't have to have broken a leg to know how to set one.

But if you have broken your leg, wouldn't you, as the physician, set it with just that much more feeling and understanding? If I break my leg, you can be sure I'm going to a doctor who has been in a cast himself. He'll know what I'm talking about when I complain of that awful itch I can't reach, and may even help me find a way to scratch it. The handicapped deserve at least as much.

§

Is This All There Is?

I never cease to be amazed at the contradictions that seem to be *life*, and especially the *American* way of life.

Our streets and highways are littered pitifully, and yet the nighttime TV ads sell cleaning products ad nauseam. Foreigners visiting us must surely think that Americans do little more than wax their floors, scrub their toilets, and shower three times a day. Yet the countryside tells them slobs live here.

The radio beats out love songs, hour after hour, extolling the virtues of love and lamenting the injustices of love-gone-wrong. Yet, we have a divorce rate approaching fifty percent. If love is so important, how come we are so lousy at it?

We enslave ourselves to the almighty dollar to buy the American dream of a house, two cars and the latest toys. Yet, when we have all these things, we want more and bigger.

And speaking of gadgets and toys: we have so many labor-saving devices that we get no exercise in the course of a day, then willingly pay hundreds of dollars a year to a health club.

After we starve and exercise ourselves to exhaustion in pursuit of thinness (i.e., lovability), we drive to the local junk food-grease-and-salt emporium for a quick meal we can stuff down while driving home from the spa! We can't take a walk at the end of the day because it isn't safe—*because* we have acquired so many goodies that others want to steal.

We are a goal-oriented culture, which is dramatized by the Olympics. With single-minded devotion, the athletes train for four years, putting all else aside for that one glorious chance to win the gold. Ah, the pursuit of the gold. It is more than just a motto for the Olympics. It seems to be an American motto.

We relentlessly pursue the gold for all it can buy in material objects, creature comforts and status. Yet when we get it, we don't seem to be happy.

I'm sure there are some happy rich people out there, but we rarely hear about them. All too often, we hear about the folks who seem to have everything, yet their lives are miserable. When there is nothing left to struggle, to sacrifice, or to dream for, relationships deteriorate, boredom sets in and discontent poisons the idle hours. As Patti Page used to croon, "*Is this all there is? Is this all there is?*"

Each day I go to work, day after day, week after week, I know that down the road, a much-deserved and much-anticipated vacation awaits. I love the planning, the saving and sacrifice. I love the final packing the night before, only to feel a strange letdown when I'm finally on vacation.

When I was a park ranger in Colorado, I met many people who felt the same. Having driven nonstop for hours just to go camping in a wilderness park, they became totally lost and unable to adjust to the sudden pace of *being there.*

The goals we set out in front of us, like the proverbial dangling carrot, are really only the motivators. It is the process, the getting there that is the key that offers the real gratification.

Working becomes the addiction, not the house or boat or car. Running becomes the fix and remains so even when the body is hard and sinewy. Olympic athletes stay on a training schedule even after the Games have closed.

Dieting becomes a way of life. Falling in love never loses its magic even when you're on your third or fourth or tenth divorce. Houses get cleaned every week whether they need it or not. The mountain climber scales the ultimate peak only to reach the summit and look across the valley to another mountain beckoning seductively.

Does this then mean that a secret to life may be that it is it not the hand that is dealt you, but that you play it? How well you play it may be the only really important thing. If so, then the setting of goals is important only as a means to an end and that the end is really the means by which we travel the road of life, no matter what the direction.

§

Hey! Pay Attention!

"Mom, Mom...Moooommmmmm!" The call of a child trying to get his mother's attention is familiar to everyone. If his repetitive calls don't work, then he will try a tug at her hand or skirt. Hey! Pay attention! If that doesn't do the trick, then a slap at her side or even a tantrum will probably be next. Whatever it takes to get a mom's attention is employed. The child's efforts will escalate until something works, even if it results in a scolding.

This pattern of escalation is not confined to children's attention-getting techniques, nor is it exclusively a character- istic of communication between two people. The one person you talk to more than any other is yourself, even when you know better.

In fact, I think most of us have become so accustomed to ignoring our inner voice, or questioning it, and assuming that someone else, anyone else, knows more than we do, that it takes a great deal to refocus our outward attention back in to ourselves. The purpose of escalation is to find what gets our attention and helps us to tune in to ourselves.

The inner voice (your unconscious, your heart, your soul) has a way of insisting that you tune in to yourself and learn certain lessons before you can move on. If you feel stuck in your life, or if things just seem to be slowly falling apart, it is probably because they are.

Your inner voice has been saying, "Hey! Pay attention!" but you haven't been listening. If you didn't pay attention early on when you stubbed your toe, then you probably got hit. If that didn't work you probably got shoved. What's next? Falling on your face, literally? Figuratively? Both? Let me give you a personal example of this kind of inner escalation that finally got my attention.

Having been a mental health professional for years, I was an excellent giver of help to others, but had not realized how lousy I was at taking any help. I could advise others that they must learn to give and take, but I could not do it myself. After all, giving and taking were the basis for involvement with others. My involvements were clearly one-sided.

"Hey! Pay attention!" my inner voice was saying. "Listen to your own good advice." I did not. I left my mental health job and worked in the business world at minimum pay.

"Hey! Pay attention! You're going to need help soon." I turned a deaf ear and used up my savings.

"Hey! Pay attention! Now you need help." Not me; I resisted. I have credit, I'll get a loan. I did. The money ran out.

"Hey! Pay attention! Now you are in trouble." I started to listen but only barely. Then, suddenly, inexplicably, I developed a crippling back problem. I literally could not drive, walk, shop, cook, do laundry or anything else.

"Hey! Pay attention! Let others give to you!" I did. I had to, but it took financial impoverishment and physical immobility to get my attention and learn about the *taking* half of giving. From that point on, my back improved and money was no longer a problem.

Now, don't get caught up in my example. Your own lessons may be quite different. The point here is that you need to pay attention to yourself, and now, so that further escalation will not be necessary. The squeaky wheel need not fall off before it gets greased. Growing need not be painful. Anthony Quinn said in *Zorba, the Greek*, "Life is trouble, only death is not." I'm telling you, "It ain't necessarily so!" But hey, you'd better pay attention!

§

The Not-So-Terrible Twos

As I looked up from my Sunday paper, which I always read at the laundromat, I met the wide-eyed stare of a little boy who had paused in his exploration of my clothes basket. I smiled and said, "Hi, are you having fun?"

"No!" he blurted back at me.

"Eddie, be nice to the lady," his embarrassed mother scolded, as she hurried to retrieve her son.

"No," he shouted again as he fought her hold, "*No, No!*"

"Hmmmmmm," I said half aloud, "he must be a two-year-old." His mother heard me and nodded yes, her eyes gratefully acknowledging that I seemed to know about the ordeal she was enduring of late.

The Terrible Two's were so tagged because as the child reaches out for his first taste of independence, he does so with ferocity, making adults nervous.

The two-year-old is unabashed about mastering his life. By the second year, he is eating whole foods and feeding himself, sharing his food generously with his clothes, the furniture, the floor, any passerby and the family pet. Still, he *is* feeding himself.

The gross motor skills of walking and running come next, along with the first experimentations with language. By his second birthday, the two-year-old's legs give him the means to explore his world, each trip carrying him further and further from the safety and confines of mother's arms.

With the acquisition of the proclamation "No" and its implications, the two-year-old has his first lesson in power. It is exhilarating, and, like a sailor with shore leave, the two-year-old can't get enough of this intoxicant. "No, no, no!"

Because he hasn't the socialization, conscience, or language to soften, qualify or explain his "No's," they stand alone, simple, pure and powerful. Even mothers, who wield the only true power in this world, can't get away with a simple, pure "No." The closest they can get is to wear a T-shirt that says, "Because I'm the Mommy, that's why!"

Two-year-olds don't think being two is terrible. They think it's *terribly wonderful*. Only adults call two-year-olds terrible and do you know why? Because two-year-olds get to do what no adult can. He can say "No" without having to justify it in any way to either himself or others. Furthermore, the two-year-old gets to say "No" when no is the truth.

"Isn't that a nice present?"

"No."

"Wouldn't you like to go play?"

"No."

"Are you having a good time?"

"No!"

He doesn't have to lie to be polite, assuage guilt, or keep from rocking the boat. The reason we adults call two-year-olds terrible is because they get away with what we can't.

I've been envying two-year-olds lately as I struggle to walk the administrative executive's tightrope of being a diplomat while still saying "No" to exploiting, manipulating, and whining customers. The two-year-old doesn't have to be a diplomat. He doesn't care whether anyone likes him or not when he says "No." His parent's opinions are the only ones that count. Social ostracism be damned. The two-year-old couldn't care less. How I envy that freedom!

How can such a little word be so hard to say and mean? Who has said "No" to you lately and been able to look you straight in the eye and not mumble any number of excuses in apologetic justification? To whom have you said "No" lately without waves of guilt diluting your resolution?

I wanted to be a grownup for as long as I can remember. When I looked at that two-year-old last Sunday, I realized what I had lost.

§

Have You Hugged Your Plants Today?

"Short of Aphrodite, there is nothing lovelier on this planet than a flower, nor more essential than a plant." Thus begins Peter Tompkins and Christopher Bird's remarkable book, *The Secret Life of Plants.*

Though it was published in 1972, I only recently discovered this book and was spellbound by it. It is a historical review of centuries of scientific research on the physical, emotional and spiritual relations between plants and man. The authors went to the Library of Congress and dusted off the secrets of plant research long buried on the archive shelves, some for centuries, by the authorities of the day.

These authors began their book with the research that originally stirred their own curiosity, something called the "Backster Response." In 1966 Cleve Backster, America's foremost lie detector expert, hooked up the electrodes of one of his lie detectors to his dracaena. That simple act of curiosity radically affected his life, and may have equally affected the planet. Backster's discovery, that plants appear to have feelings and even to read the human mind, caused strong and varied reactions around the world, in spite of the fact that Backster only claimed to have uncovered what had been known and forgotten.

From the beginnings of recorded time, man has been fascinated by, and in commune with, plants. Early research was as primitive as the tools available at the time, and many conclusions were drawn only from patient, meticulous observations.

But in the 1700s and 1800s, when more objective scientific measuring devices were invented, the research with plants moved out of the realms of conjecture, faith, and mysticism and into the world of hard, scientifically verifiable evidence. Despite these carefully executed experiments and the extensive, independent replication of the discoveries to further objectify the data, the discoveries that plants feel, move, react, and even speak, were quickly buried in archival vaults lest the accepted theories of the day be overturned and with them the power of men who pretended to honor intellectual curiosity.

As I read this book, I was gratified to know that all these years of greeting my plants had not been in vain, nor did it mean I was a little cracked. My instinct to communicate with other living organisms was now scientifically proven to be a major factor in my "green thumb."

Now, mind you, I am one of those people who do more than just say "Hello" to her plants. I greet them by name *and* tell them how gorgeous they are. I have "relationships" with my plants and guess what? Centuries of august scientists say that is exactly what is needed if your plants are to flourish. All the expertise, watering and fertilizing will not cut it, if you don't really love your plants.

Furthermore, this emotional plant "food" can be enhanced by music, the romantic or classical kind, not acid rock. Honest! Does it sound familiar? I seem to flourish under the same "feeding" routine. Don't all living things?

How come such an obvious truth is so threatening that even hard-core research proving this truth must be hidden in the back wards of university archives?

I guess we're more afraid to appear foolish than we are willing to stand in the light of knowledge that doesn't fit existing molds. I have a big fig tree that is being cared for by a friend. He does not talk to plants, nor could I persuade him to start. To get my tree the attention it needed, I found a solution and left this homespun jingle as an explanation for my friend:

"Roses are red

Violets are blue.

My fig tree is lonely;

Oh, what shall I do?

I give it lots of love,

In word and thought,

But I cannot come over,

As often as I ought.

Then I spy an old radio,

Wanting to be heard.

So I bring it to my fig tree,

To sing like a bird.

Now, if you think I am crazy,

You are probably right.

But, what does it matter,

If my tree grows tall and bright!"

Have you hugged your plants today?

§

The Ugly Swan . . .

As a child, one of my favorite stories was *The Ugly Duckling.* That story was the fragile thread I tied my hopes to as I dreamed of someday becoming a beautiful, desirable, even famous star of stage and screen. Tomboy that I was, I did have these secret fantasies that made the ugly, awkward years of latency and adolescence more bearable. There was a light at the end of that dark tunnel of growing up; *The Ugly Duckling* said so.

While waiting for an appointment the other day, I leafed casually through one of those weekly gossip magazines that specialize in the lives of the rich and famous. The candid and not very flattering childhood photos of a Hollywood beauty queen caught my eye. The captions told it all.

Though clearly rated a beauty as an adult, the woman still saw herself as basically plain, if not ugly, and she gave all credit for her beauty to her skill with make-up and the right clothes. The way she saw herself as a child was really the way she saw herself as an adult. She was just more skilled at fooling everyone into thinking she was beautiful. This star would never allow photos of her at home *au natural* because she was afraid the truth would come out: that she was really an ugly duckling in swan's plumage.

Now what I am talking about here is the old adage that first impressions are the most lasting. However, the implications are profound when you reflect on one's own first impressions. Self-image, formed early in life, endures over time in spite of evidence to the contrary.

In other words, how a child feels about himself from his earliest encounters with adults and the world will, in fact, be how he feels about himself all through his life. All of this is stock psychological theory, but let's look a little closer.

If a male child, for example, forms the opinion that he is basically a "scaredy-cat," and this image is reinforced by a macho father who doesn't believe boys should cry or feel fear, then this boy may spend his life trying to prove to himself, and to others, that he is not a coward.

He may become a supermacho male, taking innumerable risks, testing himself in the sport, auto, or romance arenas, all in service of this early self-image of being a coward. The deeper his secret belief is the more extreme in number and kind will be his attempts to prove otherwise.

If you could get this man's man to sit down and really look at why he seems to need to test his manhood constantly, you would hear him say that he hates weakness and cowardice, and fears it in himself. Maybe his father was right all those years ago, that he was nothing but a scaredy-cat, a baby, a wimp.

The constant need to test and prove himself was just window dressing. Underneath lives a scared little boy. All the acts of genuine bravery and strength are just that, acts to fool everyone, most of all himself.

You might want to say to this man, "Yes, but what about that time when you saved that child? What about all those trophies? What about what everyone thinks of you now?" Our hero waves all these accolades off, discounting them, not with modesty, but with very real disbelief that any of those things really count.

Like our beauty queen, in spite of evidence to the contrary, our man remains convinced that his first impressions of himself are the true ones, still, after all these years of trying to change the truth.

The point here is that we all form opinions of ourselves early in life and set about to change that image for the better. We spend countless hours, days, weeks, and years working to improve ourselves, yet we never believe we really succeed. In spite of concrete evidence to the contrary, we persist in our reformation efforts. We do not believe we are really different than we were as children; we just believe we fake it better.

Mirror, mirror on the wall, am I not beautiful, or brave, or smart after all?

§

The Hidden Price of Free Gifts

Ellen Goodman, a columnist for the Boston Globe, once wrote a column about one of the biggest lies parents tell their children. That lie is that "the gift of life" was free, a pure gift of love. Hidden beneath all the layers of altruistic protestations of unqualified love lurked the truth, that someday those children were expected to take care of their aging parents in exchange for the "free" gift of life (and all the other gifts such as education and medical care).

This sobering insight had evolved from Goodman's discussions with friends who, now in middle age, were flanked by adolescent children needing them less and aging parents needing them more. Trips to the pediatrician's office were now replaced by trips to the office of the gerontology specialist.

The guilt of being a working mother was now replaced by the guilt of being a working child whose parent needed them to be more available. Trips to look at prospective colleges were combined with trips to look at retirement homes and communities.

While couched in terms of children and parents, the question she was raising was a sobering one. Is there any gift of any kind that is given freely, given without a hidden price tag?

Armchair philosophers are often heard to say, "There are two kinds of people in the world, givers and takers." Takers, of course, are thought to be the more selfish of the two, but I wonder. A taker after all, says very clearly, "I need, I want," and in that respect is more honest than the giver who gives while all the time indirectly, even unconsciously, calculating what his gift will get him in return.

We all know of parents who smother their children with gifts, or lovers who smother their loves with *objects d'amour*, or individuals who smother their friends with proof of their friendship. Then when those children, lovers or friends seem ungrateful or even rejecting, the givers are hurt and mystified as to why their generosity was so used, if not abused.

It rarely occurs to the giver that he may have been using his gifts to indebt the receiver to him, thus insuring he will be given to in return.

Aging parents fear their children will abandon them. The lover fears rejection as does the friend. So we try to cement the ties that bind with proofs of love and deservedness. "I deserve your love; look at all I have done for you."

For years I have touted myself as a giver, often lamenting how many takers we givers seem to attract. Woe is me. My self-pity is highly developed. Then I got rejected by a friend I had given much to, but this time instead of crying in my beer, I got mad. Then I noticed I was overly angry and that my accusatory finger also had a fist of three fingers pointing right back at me.

Carol, ole gal, me thinks thou protests too much. Could I be the real culprit here? I listened to myself as I ranted and raved. "How could I be rejected? Look at all I've done, given, cared for this friend! Why I'm the Girl Scout oath personified! This friend ought to be more grateful if not outright cherish me!"

So there it was, in my own words. All I had given should have earned me gratitude and loyalty, if not love. What's the use of guilt if it doesn't get you something? Well it did! The burden of my overgiving had incurred such a huge debt that only rejection could cancel it. Ouch! The truth hurts.

My giving had so many hidden strings attached that eventually the only way to stop me was to cut me loose altogether. What a painful lesson I had to learn.

The lesson is not to stop giving to others, but to be honest, painfully honest, with yourself about the hidden price tags you attach to that giving. Wherever possible, cut some of those price tags off. My scissors have gotten a lot of use lately.

§

My Love/Hate Affair with the Purse

I have just purchased my eleventh big purse. I just don't seem to be able to find the perfect bag. I am sure there is a message in this endless search for the pouch that will hold everything I want it to without needing wheels or a dolly in order to take it with me.

I have taken a survey of all the bags I have around my house to see what has been right about them and what was wrong enough that I retired it for yet another.

There are cloth bags and canvas, woven hemps and lightweight synthetics, but mostly there are leather bags. How I do love the feel of leather and the patina of old, well-traveled leather. My latest purchase is the softest leather bag I have ever found.

The reason I like big bags is because I carry all kinds of things just in case I will need them or someone else might. I learned that from my mother.

Mothers can always be counted on to have extra Kleenex, aspirin, a safety pin, a stick of gum, ChapStick, a Matchbox car for their sons, and bits and pieces of Barbie costumes for their daughters. I even know a mother who, as a last resort, would look in her purse for her missing kid!

In my own mother's case, in addition to the above, she also carried extra golf tees, a golf ball or two, score cards and her golf glove, having forgotten to stuff it in her golf bag at the end of the game.

There were vitamins, a toothbrush, hand lotion, band-aids, the program from last night's symphony, letters to be mailed and bills to write. We could always count on her having an odd assortment of candy that lived more or less permanently in the bottom of her bag, and sugar cubes she inevitably, and to my father's chagrin, stole from restaurants for our horses.

Of course, her bag was smallish and could never be closed. She tried to shut it once but the zipper broke and that was that. The open, gaping purse just invited more to be stuffed into it, and it was.

She was my role model so now I have a purse like hers, except I like mine to close. Consequently, it must be bigger to hold all my necessities, sans the sugar cubes. I don't think they even make sugar cubes anymore, do they?

My purse, in addition to the usual pharmacy items, also carries a small, leather (of course) folio containing writing paper for my habitual journal-keeping, and a collection of articles I find here and there that I want to save or give to someone else.

Often, my purse will contain my portable word processor. It is a wonderful gadget and is what I am writing this column on in a motel where I am staying overnight. Those of you who have read my earlier column on insisting on wearing comfortable shoes know I walk in my Rockports and only don high heels when absolutely necessary. Those heels are also thrust into my bag.

I am currently on a diet, so I have to carry my vitamins, emergency supply of munchies, sweetener, lemon juice packets, salad dressing packets, small cans of chicken and my unleavened bread.

I had this bag thusly packed on a trip not too many weeks ago and stopped for a lunch-time tour of the local art museum. That darn bag was so heavy I had to lengthen the strap so I could *walk* the bag, letting it rest on the floor as I stopped before each display. I probably should go next to a backpack, but then I'd only add more junk to it and get a backache.

This need to carry so much with me just in case I or someone else may need something feels like trying to be all things to all people. I think women often suffer from that belief. When you become a wife and mother it is even worse since you have to try to anticipate your husband's needs and your children's.

I hate lugging my big purse all over the place. It is heavy, cumbersome and indelicate to say the least, but I have tried the small purse regimen to no avail. I just can't seem to get along without my portable home away from home. You have heard of a man or woman for all seasons? Well, I have a purse for all seasons, occasions, emergencies and locations.

Maybe the problem is I just feel more secure knowing I can patch my make-up, fix my split seam, feed my tummy, write when the inspiration strikes me, or kill a stray hour with a book and still look the proper lady, minus the clodhoppers, when I reach my destination. Now, what I need is a bag with retractable wheels!

§

SUMMER

§

It Was One of Those Days, You Know?

After a hectic morning in the office where I work, the pace slowed. The secretaries and I sat down to a leisurely cup of coffee and conversation. Ah, conversation, the balm of life. Here was my first chance of the day to exchange pleasantries, swap *men* stories, catch up on whose kids were doing what and, if I were lucky, debate a larger issue or two.

The first few minutes were as expected. Live-in boyfriend, "you know," has been ugly, "you know," since his university classes had begun and now, "you know," the landlord was selling the house and they needed to find new quarters, "you know." Her ten-year-old daughter was down with the autumn flu, "you know," which mysteriously appears at the end of each summer vacation, and some of our clients, "you know," can never be pleased even if you, "you know," stand on your head for them. "You know, they just don't appreciate you. You know?"

Now *that* I did know, but all the stuff preceding that comment, I didn't know and my ears were ringing with all the "you knows," you know what I mean?

I quickly gave up my desire for a conversation and retreated to my mountains of paperwork, you know? Ah ha! You see, even I'm doing it now. It's like catching a cold.

Before you know it, you are sneezing "you knows" right and left, backward and forward, but no one is saying "Excuse you" or "God bless you" or "Gesundheit," or even, "My poor dear, what have you caught?"

This last would probably be the most appropriate, for it does strike me as more of a disease or illness that, while not fatal, is certainly debilitating to the art of articulation.

If it is true that you are what you eat, then can it not also be true that you are what you speak? I have long held that the language one uses can tell anyone listening much more about you at that moment than the actual content of your sentences. For example:

When you are angry, you can either be extremely articulate and spew out words in a stream that cuts like the proverbial knife or, like most of us, you can stutter and stammer, wanting to say all kinds of nasties that your childhood training, guilt and conscience won't allow.

Then there are some people who don't tell you they are angry. They don't cut you up with their razor-sharp tongues, nor do they sputter like a steam engine gone awry. Instead, in the normal course of daily chitchat, they pepper their conversation with angry words, most commonly swear words.

Cussing is anger. It is not, as many would have you believe, just a bad habit. We use angry words when we are angry, and there are lots of people who are very angry all the time. They slap you with these offensive, four-letter words and you don't even know, "you know," that you are being assaulted.

"God d.... it, all to h..., anyway. What the h... is going on here?" and so on. These words aren't even fit to print, yet we take them for granted and even ignore them in every day conversation, readily tagging those who take offense to be old fuddy duddies and of another generation. "You know?"

And what does swearing have to do with this banal expression, "you know?" It offends me, just as swearing offends me. Its use, two, three and more times in a sentence is as irritating to listen to as a sentence punctuated with cussing, because the speaker can't or won't expand his vocabulary to more expressive terms with more precise meanings. Using "you know" is like swearing. It is lazy, sloppy, and insulting to your listener because it assumes he or she cannot understand anything more complicated. There is also a hidden hostility to the expression, for to say to your listener, "you know," all the time is to say, "You know what I am telling you, but I'm going to tell you anyway and waste your time while I grind your sensibilities."

When I hear a person using "you know" repeatedly, I suddenly realize that he has ceased to listen to himself and therefore must have ceased listening to anyone else. It is true that a new, cool way of talking such as, "Hey, you know, man, like wow," can soon become a stale bad habit.

Bad habits are hard to break, but since when do we give in to bad habits and go on our merry way expecting everyone in our path to be forgiving and accepting of "where we're at man, you know?"

I go through periods of swearing every now and then and know that I am angry and need to pay attention. And like the cold, if you can't find the cause right away, at least you can attack the symptoms.

The eight-year-old son of my boss, as bright a kid as you could hope to meet, has caught this "cold" of "you knows." The cause, of course, was the adult example all around him. It wasn't my place to correct him, but I did since I speak the English language and hoped to speak it with him. I kept after him to delete his "you knows" and eventually it worked. He is now a joy to talk with, for there is nothing prettier than the English language spoken properly, you know?

§

Some Days I Would Rather Be an Animal

"Mieux que jeconnais les hommes, plus j'aime mon chien." This was the slogan on a T-shirt I once owned. Translated it means, "The more I know about men, the more I like my dog." It is meant to be a feminist dig, but I would like to change it just a little. "Mieux que jeconnais l'homme, plus j'aime mon chien." The more I know about *man*, the more I like my dog. For indeed, the more I see of man, the more I admire the animal kingdom and its instinctual limitations.

In most cases animals don't fight to the death, only to the point of dominance over the nearest rival in their social group, species and geographic territory. Man, on the other hand, aims for and often succeeds in, dominating men of many classes, races, social groups and across geographic boundaries with weapons designed to maim and kill.

The present D-Day memorials are poignant reminders of man's need to dominate. The overt and covert arms race is even more absurd. What will all the extra bombs be needed for when the first few have wiped out the human race? How many times can you kill someone? The experts say the arms race is a complex issue to understand and on one level no doubt it is. On another level, I think you can see its etiology right here in "River City."

Recently, I was at an intersection waiting to make a left turn. My view was blocked by the line of cars facing me trying to make their left turn. Suddenly, I became aware of someone screaming at me. The driver of a pickup truck behind me was screaming at me to turn. He apparently could see from his higher vantage point.

I was tempted to be goaded into a careless move, but resisted in spite of the continuing harangue now peppered with profanity. Regrettably, I then sank to his level and told him to shut up and drive his own car. We made the turn and my tormentor pulled up alongside me so he and his two companions could bellow in my face. I confess, I sank even further at that point and gave a hand gesture that could not be mistaken.

How easily we can be pulled down by the baseness of others! In one final effort to exert his supremacy, the driver gunned his 1959 decrepit pickup and sped ahead of me. It was pathetic really. If you are going to out-accelerate someone on the road, you'd think you would have a turbo-something-or-other to do it in and be truly impressive.

Being a coward at heart, I ducked into a nearby parking lot. I did not want to repeat the performance at the next light or risk escalating into a physical confrontation I would surely lose. I was outnumbered, outweighed, and outclassed in the profanity department.

I also needed to calm myself from such an intensely hostile encounter with total strangers for no good reason. There I was making a left turn at a light, minding my own business, and within five minutes a little mini-war had started. How easily we could have come to blows!

I have another example. Watch what happens the next time you stop at a traffic light and stop next to another car. Do you not get into a silent and subtle competition of inching forward so your bumper is just ahead of his? Taking turns, you crowd the light like racehorses in a starting gate.

The light turns, and the contest to be the fastest out into the intersection is on. How competitive we are. How aggressive in arenas of no consequence. Animals compete for the privilege of procreation. They growl to communicate, not to insult and degrade. When we want to insult someone, we say, "He acts like an animal." If only humans *would* act more like animals, we would be selectively aggressive, in arenas that count, and therefore not be on the road to nuclear extinction.

§

My Old Shoe Friendship

Deep in the recesses of my clothes closet, down behind a couple of discarded shoeboxes, down under a much used canvas carryall, down beneath some long-forgotten winter hats and gloves, is my favorite pair of shoes. They're covered with the dust and dirt I neglected to clean off the last time I wore them. The rawhide laces are stiff from neglect, and the knots where they had broken on some long-forgotten hike feel petrified into stone. Still I refuse to throw them out.

This particular pair of shoes is made of thick leather with indestructible soles to withstand hours and days of walking, which they do admirably. The sides and toes have stretched to conform to all the irregularities of my foot.

By virtue of their position in my closet, it is obvious that I don't wear these old walking shoes much anymore, but there was a day when I wore no others. Still, even now, when I put them on it feels as if I've never had them off, and we go out into the world as confidently and comfortably as we ever did.

I consider this pair of shoes a dear old friend, and it often reminds me of a dear old human friend as well. Like the shoes, this friend and I don't get together much anymore since she married and moved hundreds of miles away. And like my walking shoes, she and I were once inseparable and viewed the world as our oyster. Together we could walk miles without tiring. Together we could talk without running out of topics, and we never felt any discomfort.

We met horseback riding in the mountains around Santa Fe. She has hair cascading down her back to her hips, is tall and slender, and is the epitome of an *earth mother*. Her face is never disguised behind make-up, and she favors long flowing dresses made from natural fabrics in designs from the Middle Ages. On anyone else, this style would seem discordant with the twentieth century, but for this woman, it fits. She has a timelessness about her as if she belongs to all the ages of man and to all of mankind.

Once, as I returned to New Mexico from a summer as a national park ranger in Colorado, I stopped to visit this friend. If I had not known her exact address, I could have driven the streets of Santa Fe and known her house when I saw the garden.

The entire front yard was planted in concentric circles overflowing with cornstalks and green beans intermingled among the zinnias, marigolds, bluebells and roses. The footpaths were bordered with a profusion of herbs and spices that would dry as they hung from the kitchen vigas all winter. The flowers attracted the bees which pollinated all the other plants. Ladybugs controlled the aphids, and only compost fertilized the soil. The sight and smell of it was intoxicating.

At first, I didn't see my friend as I gazed in awe at the garden, but there she was, standing barefoot in the womb of her creation, watering each plant and beaming from ear to ear, enjoying my reaction. It was why she had planted it in the first place.

To look at us, my friend and me, you would not guess us to be friends. We look nothing alike. She is the original flower child of the Sixties and I am an Ivy League, preppie pretender. I wear muted earth tones in tweed, khaki, camel hair and twill. My shoes are pumps or penny loafers, and my sweaters are properly monogrammed. I admire my friend's grace and the ease with which she dons her sandals, sheer Indian cotton blouses (braless, of course), and ankle-length wraparound skirts.

My hair is cut short and precisely, while her mane sweeps over her shoulders unencumbered by clips or barrettes, or it may rest on her spine in a single braid which is never secured with a rubber band at the tip.

This friend of mine is the strongest woman I know, both physically and spiritually, and unashamedly so. While the rest of us try to tone down our strengths to avoid appearing too intimidating to our male counterparts, this woman seems to strut her stuff without apology or offensive pride.

My favorite pair of shoes is like my friend, and she is like my shoes. At first glance we do not seem to go together. The shoes are not fashionable, crisp, proper or the correct image for a preppie. They are earth shoes, that is, shoes in which one may really walk and therefore know the earth. I have come to know the earth at my friend's side as well.

My shoes are unadorned with buckles and bows. Their beauty is in their simplicity. My friend is thusly beautiful as well. My shoes are made of thick durable leather, hand-stitched and soled for long years of wear and tear. My friend is made of durable stuff, too. She is strong and patient, tough yet tender, and joins the different fabrics of her life with the careful attention of a weaver, which she is. She, too, has endured the years of wear and tear, and our friendship has weathered many a sojourn.

My shoes have, over long days of walking, molded to my feet and the idiosyncrasies of my stride. My friend accepts my peculiarities just as I accept hers. We wear well together.

To the outsider we look like an odd couple, a mismatch if there ever was one, but inside we are harmonious souls, each singing in a different octave, but melodious companions nevertheless.

Some old friends, like some old shoes, can never be discarded. Time and circumstance may take us away from daily encounters, but the "fit" is never lost.

§

The Best Sex—Verbal Intercourse

Every time I walk by a newsstand or pass through a grocery store check-out line, I am interested and alarmed to note headline after headline extolling the virtues of sex. If you only knew the right steps, tricks, positions, and attitudes, you could cure whatever ails your sex life and thus save your marriage, keep your lover, or attract the mate of your dreams.

I don't believe it and neither should you. Since when has a recipe for behavior ever worked on human beings for long, if at all? Such recipes are, of course, the very meat and potatoes of behavioral therapies in the world of psychology. With simple problems, to a limited degree, they can help. You can cope with your shyness better if you make yourself socialize once a week. What you are getting are experiences that build the self-confidence and social skills you somehow didn't get earlier.

But sex? The attention it gets renders it positively boring. Why, you would think it was the most important thing that happens between two people. It is not. Talking is. I don't mean the "Hi, how are you. Nice weather we're having" kind of talking. Like sex, you can do that with a stranger and not remember the encounter ten minutes later.

I'm talking about *talking,* the kind that's eyeball to eyeball. This is how I feel; tell me how you feel. I'll risk letting you see my vulnerabilities if you'll trust me, too, kind of talking.

Think about it. Isn't the best sex the kind that happens after you are friends, so you aren't embarrassed or even self-conscious about your less than "10" physique? Isn't the best sex the kind that is paced so there is fun, laughter, and banter, as well as passion? Isn't the best sex when you lie awake for hours talking softly, letting your hearts go naked because your bodies are and it's comfortable to be so?

How many times have you glanced at a member of the opposite sex and thought him (or her) divine? As divine providence would have it, your paths cross. Oh, be still my pounding heart. It obeys as soon as he (she) opens his mouth. Bad breath and inanities come falling out like so many autumn leaves floating to the ground, pretty but dead! So much for the wonders of chemistry!

Tell me, you long-marrieds, is it passion, the kind that only Hollywood can produce, that makes you love your mate year in and year out, or is it friendship, spawned of long hours of talking out the problems of daily life together?

And tell me, you once- or many-times divorced folk, if you had to sum it all up in one sentence, would you not say, "We just didn't, couldn't, wouldn't talk to each other like we used to, should have, or longed to?"

Why do psychotherapy, counseling, confessions, and prayer work so effectively? It is because they all provide that someone to listen to you, talk to you, and accept you for who and what you are, wrinkles, fat, foibles and all.

You could say of psychotherapy, counseling, confessions and prayer that they are truly intimate experiences. In each, one may speak from the heart and reveal the most feared and shameful corners of oneself. Dreams, too, are whispered and not mocked. Tears are shed and not ridiculed. Anger is vomited without recrimination.

When you really want to be intimate with someone, you want to touch that person's heart and mind with your words, your eyes *and* your fingertips. How's that for a recipe?

§

American Guilt over Money

Watching the American society struggle with its ambivalence over money is a fascinating and enduring drama. Perhaps because this nation was settled primarily by immigrants, the common man fleeing the yoke of aristocratic suppression, the average American seems to simultaneously love and hate money.

The perennial debate over income taxes is as good a stage as any to watch this ambivalence at work. Fairness is the hue and cry of the President and everyone else jumping on the tax reform bandwagon at election time. The battle lines are drawn between the privileges of the few and the welfare of the many. Those privileged few came to America (or their ancestors did) seeking the same golden opportunities the many did, yet now they are viewed with hostility as if they were the direct descendants of European aristocracy.

This fascination with and repugnancy toward the very rich is clearly reflected on television with the huge success of the nighttime soaps such as *Dynasty* and *Dallas* and their successors. The American public cannot seem to get enough of watching these people at work and play, yet these same people in real life are seen as the villains just because they have been better at dealing with money and the system than the rest of us. What inspires admiration of television characters seems to turn to envy and revulsion in real life.

The American dream is one of rags-to-riches, so the self-made millionaire is an okay guy because he *earned* every penny and thereby deserves his wealth. Those who inherit great wealth are not so deserving it seems. Their money came too easily, and they did not give blood, sweat or tears for it.

Easy money is the money of the aristocracy and hard money is the money of the working man and therefore, is more honest. Yet Jack Kennedy's money was inherited. He didn't work for it. But when he became the political champion of the poor, his easy money was washed clean in the waters of altruism, and we could all then feel justified in our fascination with Camelot.

In any other context, a monarchy or the semblance of a monarchy is not tolerated in this country, as Richard Nixon found out. Our ancestors came here to get away from the tyranny of the ruling classes. Yet the American people spend the majority of their time pursuing the level of wealth that will allow them to live like kings.

And while they take pride in being hard-working common men, they spend hundreds and thousands of dollars in the sweepstakes and lotteries just for the chance at some quick, easy money. Everyone wants to be an instant millionaire, yet berates those who do become instantly rich through inheritance or apparent overnight success.

In this country, easy money is bad money, and money that comes the hard way is good money. Lucky money, as in sweepstakes wealth, must be okay money. After all, who can hold luck against you?

In Europe and the Far East, where people have always lived with and even worked to preserve the concept of aristocracy and monarchs, the people are not as impressed by money as Americans are, nor are they as embarrassed and guilty about it as we seem to be.

In championing the fairness doctrine for the struggling middle class, Reagan was trying to abdicate as the king of the upper (aristocratic) class and thereby insure his place in American history, which is the success story of the common man. America's wealth and wealthy people are a testimony to the fabulous success story that *is* America. Too bad we can't enjoy it more.

§

Honey, Darling, Buddy, Boy...

"Honey, honey, can you get me the key to room six?" asked the middle-aged woman in a high-pitched, slightly whiny voice. Walking toward the irritant, I replied, "I can if you will stop calling me 'honey.'"

The whiny retort came back, "Well, then, what shall I call you, darling?"

Despite an icy stare and the emphatic shake of my head, she dug her hole a little deeper: "It's only a figure of speech, you know."

With an arched eyebrow and a steely gaze, I said, "It's a very condescending figure of speech." The rigidity of my back said the rest.

There is nothing that irritates me more than the so-called endearing terms we so carelessly use when we are trying to mask an inner, pervasive hostility that every so often leaks out of our otherwise tight control.

Syrupy, whiny "honeys" and "darlings" for women and the overly jocular buddy or boy for men when spoken to non-intimates are terms that sound nice, but often mean the opposite.

I have often written about the inadequate ways our American society deals with anger and this is one more example. These terms are more than hostile. They are degrading and condescending, which is more hostile than nice, clean aggression. And therein may be the real meaning of such perverse application of these apparent terms of endearment.

Men are allowed to be more overtly aggressive in this society, hence do not need to use verbal subterfuge as much as women. But think of the sidewalk, barroom or football stadium encounters you have witnessed where one man approaches another with a hearty clap on the back and an exaggerated grin on his face.

"Well, ole buddy, how the heck are you?" If you are such buddies, how come he doesn't know how you are? Or "Hey boy, what's happening?" It is no mistake that the term boy was the trademark of white racism toward blacks. It is very degrading to a grown man.

Women are not allowed to be as overtly aggressive as men so they must use insidious terms like honey, sweetie and dear to unload their unladylike feelings.

My condescending tormentor cast her hostility in stone the very next morning. Seeing me, she made a beeline for the only man in the office at that time.

"Sir...Oh, sir? Can you help me?"

Sir, Sir! He gets a sir and I get honey? There it was: the hostility of sexism from one of my own. Just *who is* the enemy anyway?

§

Who Wants to Grow Up Anyway?

"When did that become a rule? I've never heard of it. No one told me! 'They' didn't send *me* any official regulations."

So went the incredulous self-centered protests of an occasional university student when informed that parking stickers were required for all students. Since this guy had never heard of this rule before, he didn't think it could be so! Imagine the authorities not consulting him first. The nerve of those people!

If that wasn't bad enough, this same student was very put out that he had come to art class without the recommended drawing pad and pen.

"Just when was the information about class supplies disseminated? Did they send out a supply list? No one told *me*!"

Well, poor dear, he had registered for the art painting class by mail, paying for a course he selected by title only, and had not bothered to inquire about its content, the teacher, or anything else about it. Perhaps he thought they might paint the air with imaginary brushes. Did it occur to him to read the catalog? Did it occur to him to make inquiries?

Never mind about that. Why should he think for himself or do any of his own legwork? He was paying for this class, a whole $1.56 per hour, so by golly, they should take care of all the details he might like to know. Who wants to grow up anyway? Of course, if they had told him to buy supplies and a text, then when he got to class and didn't like it, they would be responsible again for his discontent! It's called you can't win for losing.

In running my small business, I recently had a similar experience. I state the standard 30-day term for payment on my invoices and, inevitably, the customer keeps his money as long as he can before paying. Some keep their payment past the due date, making it a policy to pay only after the past due notices start to arrive. I start making phone calls after the first one is sent out.

Recently, I called requesting payment of a bill which was 25 days delinquent and was told, "But we only got one past due notice! We always pay after the third one!" The customer was incensed that I wasn't more grateful for their promptness in paying their bill late! Who wants to grow up anyway?

I know where this attitude comes from. In business circles it's called the grace period. Credit is extended because it is presumably better to keep a late-paying customer than no customer at all, even if they cost you a fortune in postage. The point, however, is the presumptive attitude that unless *they*, the omnipresent *other*, take responsibility for us, we cannot be expected to act responsibly for ourselves.

The nine-year-old schoolboy lies in bed or dawdles in the bathroom until his mother calls at least three times. It feels so good to have her taking such good care of him. The less he does for himself, the more she will do for him. Oh, yummmmmmmm. Who wants to grow up anyway?

The customer wants your wonderful product, but, if the truth be known, he wants you to give it to him. If he drags his feet on paying for it, it will feel like the *free* gifts he got as a child. Oh boy, who wants to grow up anyway?

And the student, even at age forty-five, still refuses to think for himself. No one told him about this, that, or the other thing so he has every right to holler. Everyone knows you go to the university to be taken care of. Next to state and federal governments, schools are the institutionalization of motherhood. *They* are supposed to anticipate all your needs, questions and desires. Who *does* want to grow up anyway?!

§

Mirror, Mirror on the Wall, Who IS That After All?

The other day, a friend of mine celebrated her seventy-first birthday and we were talking about how no matter how old you get, you don't feel your age because you keep an internal image of yourself fixed in your mind. She said she is surprised when she looks in her mirror and sees this old, gray-haired lady in front of her. "Who is that woman?" she wonders. Her internal view of herself is of the thirty-five-year-old professional who was at her prime in her mid-thirties, had the world by the tail and no one could stop her.

We both wondered why it is that in all the psychology books and in all the new literature coming out about this new specialty of gerontology, no one ever writes about this phenomenon of having disparate internal and external images of oneself.

It is very curious, and I am experiencing the same thing even though the gap between my ideal self and the person I am now is not that wide. Still, I do look in the mirror and wonder who that woman is with the lines and those awful dark circles under her eyes.

I do not accept how my body is not as strong or responsive as it used to be. I need more sleep now, and I buy wrinkle creams even though doctors say they do not work. My skin is drying out and I need a short haircut to look younger.

Of late, I have been dieting and have every intention of getting down to my high school weight and size, even though reality would tell me that I have aged, spread and sagged irrevocably and all the Nordic Track cross-country exercising and swimming daily will not reverse the clock. I am going to my thirtieth (my god!) high school reunion this summer, and by golly, I want to look like the cheerleader I was in those days. Alas, the wire rim glasses that I cannot get along without will give me away. After all, I do want to *see* all those old (whoops-former) boyfriends, and I hope to make them sweat a little bit, too.

This losing weight business is tough stuff I want to tell you, which is why all those books and schemes promising you quick weight loss sell so well. However, the truth is: what you took years to put on will take at least weeks and months to take off, so you might as well just learn to appreciate losing the quarter pound. Just think of it as one more stick of butter off your bones.

I have kept this diet remarkably well, but my problem with dieting is water retention. I can look at the salt shaker and hold water, which is a real drag on the ole morale, let me tell you. However, it is coming off a stick of butter a day or so. I am getting there. Still, the image in the mirror is just not me, the *Me* I keep in my mind's eye.

She is a thirty five-year-old gal, svelte, athletically muscled, sassy and not afraid of anything. Where has that gal gone? She is not in my mirror anymore, that's for sure. Instead, staring back at me is a person who has been burned enough times to become cautious. A person who just can't dig up the garden the way she used to and needs to call a young boy to come do the heavy work; a person who goes to bed by nine o'clock with a good book instead of tripping the light fantastic; a person who has eyeglasses stashed all over the house. Before you know it, they will be hanging around my neck just to cut down on the sheer numbers of glasses I have to keep track of or go hunting for.

That wicked Queen/stepmother/witch in *Snow White* kept asking her mirror who was the fairest of them all, and that old mirror did not lie. I guess my mirror isn't lying either.

§

My Mother Never Warned Me!

I have read and re-read Gail Sheehy's works *Passages* and *Pathfinders*. The study of growing older and the stages we go through had been going on for years before Sheehy brought it to the public's attention and put it in terms we could readily understand. Yet, I find myself surprised that I am growing older. What makes it worse is that I taught developmental psychology for years. Still, it hadn't prepared me for this thing call aging.

The theories I know. I can quote chapter and verse from the experts about what happens physically and psychologically at thirty, forty, fifty and sixty, but to see myself standing in the middle of the puddle of midlife with my feet wet and a bit muddy is a shock.

First of all, somewhere along the line, I got the idea that life would get easier the older I got. It doesn't. In fact, it's harder and certainly more complicated. As a kid, I had all I could do trying to grow up and learn the physical, social and academic skills society demanded of me.

Now, as an adult, I have to keep all those skills finely honed and adapt them to a seemingly endless variety of people and situations I walk, stumble, or back into without knowing it. Everyone else's feelings have to be taken into account and I almost never get to do what I want even when I declare that is what I am going to do!

Secondly, the physical aches and pains are unexpected and unwelcome. I am not the least bit tolerant of early morning stiffness, of my legs falling asleep after only a short time in one position, of swollen ankles at the end of the day or of thinking the bed especially inviting by nine at night.

When your grandparents die you grieve, for in their passing you know that your childhood is over, but still your parents live and are still older than you. They stand between you and the grim reaper as a protective barrier.

Then before you know it, you're the next generation to face death. Barring accidents and catastrophic illness, you reach that point where you have at least as much past as you have future. Phrases like "remember when" and "in our day" creep into your conversational repertoire. You are no longer somebody's kid. You are the adult, the parent, the senior vice-president in the firm called life.

Now you buy birthday cards for your friends and they for you that say, "You're not getting older, just better, more experienced, wiser." Total strangers call you ma'am and sir. Health and diets for longer life instead of for beauty become fascinating topics.

Health spas charge big fees because they cater to the people who are old enough to be making big bucks. Men start jogging, pumping iron and wearing gold chains around their necks when they don shirts opened to the navel to show their hairy or not-so-hairy chests. Women buy wrinkle and spot removal creams, have long acrylic nails put on and join Jazzercise classes. At least I'm not alone.

No longer can I trip the light fantastic, though I still try occasionally. No longer can I eat and drink anything I want, though I still do, promising to diet on the morrow. No longer can I skip a day of walking, swimming, or biking, yet I do and get irritated when I'm stiff all over.

Most days I'd rather go to bed with a book than with a man, even though all the slick magazines tell me a little seductive effort on my part would bring back all the magic of youthful yesteryear. Some days I'm so tired, even magic doesn't interest me.

In fact, youth doesn't interest me much anymore, and I only pretend to like the music to be sociable. I like doctor's office music. It's soothing and I prefer to be soothed than to be jazzed up with a bone-shattering rock beat.

I never paid much attention to all this until my much-younger secretary switched the radio channel from my classical music while I was out of the office and then made a face at me of half sympathy and half disgust when I switched it back. I hadn't noticed that I had grown older. It seems to have happened suddenly. I wish my mother had warned me.

§

Why Pay When It Is Free?

Why should I pay for something I can get free? Why should I take the time to vote when I already live in a democracy? Why should I go to a concert or to the theater when I can turn on the TV? Why should I support a church, if God's love is free? Why indeed!

In a society dominated by money as the bottom line in everything, the "why should I pay when it's free" philosophy at first seems to make perfect pragmatic sense. But upon reflection, it does not.

What price are you willing to pay for freedom of choice? What price for quality through competition? What price for ideas?

This is an election year, and yet one of the most-often heard news items is how many people will probably not vote this year. After celebrating the 4th of July, how many people paused on that day to really think about the momentous piece of paper declaring the independence of this infant nation and the costly war it issued?

Every week we hear of suppressed people risking life and limb to be able to worship in their own church, yet our churches struggle to meet their budgets year after year.

I'm afraid we take our freedom for granted: our freedom to worship or not, our freedom to choose what we'll read, to choose what we'll listen to, to choose how we'll make our livings, to choose where we'll live, to choose to speak our minds either out loud or in writing.

We take for granted all our freedoms to choose, and even abuse them every time we refuse to exercise those choices and make whatever sacrifices are necessary to support them.

You can't keep the freedom to vote if you don't go out and do it. You must attend and support your church, museum, or concert hall if you want them to be available at all. Without choices, you don't have freedom of choice, and without freedom of choice, you don't have freedom. Just ask the Russians, the Poles or the Chinese.

The freedom to choose was the ship of hope every immigrant to America has sailed. It still is. Today on the radio was news of East Germans so desperate to come to the West that they refused to leave their hiding place to pick up promised visas. And what about all the boat people from Asia and Cuba? They aren't suffering untold hardships to come to a place where it is bad to live! For all the criticism America suffers abroad, our country still remains the brightest star in the freedom sky. Those of us who live here don't realize what we have, and it is the little abuses of freedom that will erode it until there is nothing left.

Termites don't fell a house all at once. They eat away at the base until it no longer can support the superstructure. It isn't the Presidency or even Congress that keeps the country together. It is each individual who cares enough to do whatever is needed to keep freedom alive in his own soul, his own life, his own family, social group, and town.

Freedom is not free. If you want the freedom to choose, then you must support more than one of each thing, because then and only then are you supporting the idea of choice, the idea of competition, the idea of freedom. This newspaper can be obtained free, but the idea it represents cannot.

§

Pigs in the Forest

I'm what you call an outdoor girl. My idea of a vacation is backpacking in the wilderness or river rafting down some remote tributary of an untamed river deep in the mountains. The smell of an open wood fire and dew-dampened pine needles can intoxicate me faster than any alcohol on the market. The best part of a day for me is the sunrise when the night chill is kissed away by the warming sun rays.

This past weekend I went camping with a friend from Santa Fe. We met in Socorro and headed west into the Cibola National Forest. Before we could set up camp, we had to clean up the campsite from the refuse left by previous visitors. It is so hard for me to understand the mentality of littering streets, parks, or the wilderness.

What logic, or lack of it, goes into a value system that allows a person to soil a public place without guilt of any degree? Is it just a mindless self-centeredness that blocks out any consideration for the next guy, the animals, the next generation, or is it a wanton hostility toward others and the world?

I spent one summer as a national park ranger on the North Rim of the Black Canyon of the Gunnison National Monument. I was the sole ranger in the park on that side, so I did all the daily maintenance, trail minding, tour guiding, fire marshalling, and rescuing. It was a wonderful job *except* for having to pick up the litter.

Every day I got angry about it. Even cleaning the outhouses wasn't as bad as the endless picking up the soda can pop-tops and cigarette butts. After all, cleaning privies is a straightforward affair. The users have either hit or missed, and I'm here to tell you they did miss and often! Oh, well, the space you had to clean was limited, and lots of lime worked wonders.

But litter is different. It is lightweight and blows from one campsite to the next and then across the fence boundary into the unspoiled areas. Even having to clean up just the campsites wouldn't have been so bad, but I had park visitors who chose to park overnight at the lookout points instead of at the designated camp sites.

One group of four couples were especially barbaric and purposely draped used Kotex and Tampax on bushes, sprinkled the contents of their ashtrays up and down the pathways, turned empty juice and milk cartons upside down on tree limbs, half-buried their empty liquor bottles and threw beer cans in all directions. They even left someone's vomit from the night's excesses wrapped in a towel at the information poster.

These "campers" had been so vile to me when I asked them to leave that I was frightened and reported their license plates to the command post across the canyon in case something happened to me. It wasn't just anger I felt when I had to clean up that mess, but shock as well. I could not fathom that human beings, the supposed top of the evolutionary chain, could act so despicably.

If you think alcohol makes people act unlike themselves instead of more so, you could blame the booze. Or you could cite the bitterness of racial prejudice, since five of the eight were of two different minorities. Several were grossly obese and, in our society, fat people are often treated badly. Or if you believe in reincarnation, you could say these people had simply not evolved to even a base level as yet.

Whatever your modus operandi for explaining inexplicable human behavior, there was no doubt their violence against nature was as virulent an outburst of rage as I have ever witnessed.

After that summer of rangering, the few gum wrappers and six-pack plastic rings I found on this most recent camping trip seemed inconsequential. Yet they were not.

Most things in life are on a continuum, from mild to severe. The assault on the environment of Black Canyon was only a grosser expression of the carelessly dropped gum wrapper. Both seem to say of the litterer, "I am a spoiled brat, too lazy to walk a few feet to use a trash barrel or put my hand in my pocket." These "pigs in the forest" can only see themselves as belonging to themselves rather than to the society, the human race, or the animal kingdom. The consequences of their acts do not register beyond their own needs.

§

Letting Go. . . Exquisite Agony

A couple of years ago, I had the good fortune to interview a renowned local rancher several months before he died. A century before, his father had purchased some of the family ranch at the edge of what is now the White Sands Missile Range from a James MacAlister, so he was curious about me as well.

J. C. was an avid historian, as am I, so we were in hog heaven so to speak, talking for hours about the history of our southern New Mexico home. One of the questions I asked Mr. C., as I do of every elderly person I have the privilege to interview, was "If you had one piece of advice to give to young people today, what would it be?"

He answered me with a story. When he was about ten years old, the southern half of the New Mexico territory was besieged by a long drought. The cattle were dying in large numbers. His father decided to move the herd to the Corralitos range west of Las Cruces, hoping that the rains from the west had fallen there before being stopped by the Organ Mountains. But those grasslands were parched also and now the cattle were dying by the hour.

Finally, the decision to sell was made, even though it meant starting all over again. Young James never forgot that drought or its bitter lesson of letting go. His advice to young people was, "Sell in times of drought." Translated beyond the realm of cattle ranching, his advice was to learn to cut your losses, learn to let go, learn to say goodbye. If you hang on too long, you may lose everything.

How right he was. How hard it is to let go of dreams, loves, even possessions. Old habits and customs die hard even when they no longer serve or have become destructive. Think of the marriages you know that persist, glued together by mutual contempt and hatred. Think of the employees and employers who trudge to work each day barely able to tolerate each other or the job. Why can't they let go and move on? Why do all of us have so much trouble letting go? We have had plenty of practice and yet...?

The infant must let go of the comfort of his mother's lap for the realities of the high chair, walking and grown-up food. The toddler must let go of his babyhood for the realities of siblings and school. The once ever-present blanket and thumb are replaced by a beloved doll that one day falls apart and cannot be mended. A child's pet dies and a piece of the child dies with it. Many of us have forgotten those "letting goes" until we are confronted by a child in the midst of his agony; then the old scars are painfully stretched.

In our mobile society, childhood homes and friends are lost repeatedly. When those tears are aborted prematurely, the grief work is never completed, and a corner of our hearts is left behind, locked away from any new attachment possibilities. Think of the profuse and public grieving we see almost daily on the TV from the latest Middle Eastern calamity. You'd never see such an outpouring of tears and rage in this country. Real men and superwomen don't cry. Chin up, stiff upper lip and all that, ole chap.

Letting go must not be confused with quitting, however. Being tough and having backbone was exactly what made it possible for J.C.'s pioneering family to carve out their ranch in the first place and enabled them to rebuild it after the drought. But knowing when to bend, when to let go, was also what saved them. Unbearable as it was to let the elements defeat them, in the end they were victorious. By bending, they were not broken.

It was exquisite agony to make such a decision. If you do not allow yourself to grieve fully and allow the tears, rage, and disappointment to wash through you like one of our wild western summer thunderstorms, then you will never experience the sense of renewal from an earth (and soul) freshly washed clean.

When we fail to let go, life becomes oppressive, like the dark clouds of humidity that suffocate the breezes, and adds lead weight to each step. Unspent grief prolongs your pain and will soon leak out in the form of chronic illnesses, accidents, irritability, depression, and in poor performances at home and on the job. A stiff upper lip can break your back, literally and figuratively. As this writer/poet once wrote, "I will not live in dread of the pain of farewells, but welcome it as the darkness before the dawn."

§

Endings Are Beginnings, Too

As the rain finally broke away from the confines of the thunderclouds, I was struck by the pungent aromas released from the earth. Summer thunderstorms have a wonderfully cleansing effect, washing the earth clean and refreshing the air with an abundance of natural perfumes.

The night the storm broke, I'd been reading some poetry I had written nine years before after a long-lost lover unexpectedly reappeared, tied my heart up in knots (again), and then left for his home in Europe as suddenly as he had come. In the wake of his departure, I struggled to put some semblance of order to my feelings by writing them down. As I wrote, a soft, gentle rain began to fall, and as the sky wept, so did I. Together, earth and soul were relieved of our burdens.

I am often struck with the parallels between nature and man. There are people who are like high country brooks. Shallow and energetic they bubble along, making lots of noise like children that cheer their environs.

Then there are those who are more mature, like streams which have still not mellowed into the deep and quiet rhythm of the adult river. Like adolescents, these streams can be swift and unpredictable.

Old Man River finds his strength in his depth. Of course, some rivers are not so quiet. Some pack all the excitement and danger of fast water and wild rapids. I've known a few people like that. They gave me quite a ride.

I see the human element in trees too. Like some people and many relationships, some trees can withstand the storms of life better than others. There are oaks and cottonwoods, older than remembered time. Like some people, they are seemingly indestructible. They endure no matter what comes their way. Others are of less hearty stock. Those too rigid break in the first strong wind. Others bend over low at the slightest disturbance.

Life is so daily and our efforts to survive so consuming, that it is often very hard to get any perspective on ourselves and how our lives fit into an overall picture. Some days I simply feel lost, even when all external events seem to be humming right along quite smoothly. It is at times like these that I try to step back and draw some analogies to nature.

Do I feel lost because I have just weathered a traumatic human storm and am a bit stunned to find myself still standing? Think of the aftermath of a storm in nature. Many things have been torn from their roots and carried away. Those losses create conflicting feelings of grief and relief. Things we become accustomed to also tie us down. Familiarity is safe but restrictive.

Have you ever climbed a big hill and wondered if you would ever reach the top? You become so engrossed in the climb that you almost miss noticing that you have reached your goal. For hunters, if the chase is long and hard enough, the kill almost seems anticlimactic. Some even feel a sense of disappointment, a letdown.

As the slow, hot days of summer force me into more contemplative postures, and the afternoon thunderstorms roll in offering momentary relief, I am comforted to know that man is a part of nature and that my life too has predictable rhythms and seasons. As one season or period of my life ends, that ending also signals the beginning of a new season, its character yet unknown. The mystery of what is to come is tantalizing and frightening. The storm has finally blown itself out. Now what?

§

Getting the Message

Have you ever marveled at the messages life brings you just when you need inspiration the most? Having indulged in five days of copious eating and drinking at the long anticipated family reunion, I swore a silent oath, as the airplane headed west, to go on a diet and start exercising.

In Atlanta we picked up more passengers and the two who sat down next to me turned out to be professional bodybuilders and second in the nation to boot! T. and S. were returning from a competition, and every muscle was glaring at me as if to say, "You see what you can do if you would only try!"

S. turned out to be wonderfully friendly and gregarious, so we spent our time discussing the art class I was taking (I was drawing on the plane) and how she got into body building. It seems three years ago her husband, who was already into competitive bodybuilding, found a new partner, a gorgeous blonde. S., who was fifty pounds overweight and happy as a clam tending her stable of horses on the California coast, decided that blonde was trouble. She began to work out just three times a week at home with very simple exercises. She gave them to me. I don't have to join a spa now.

As it happened, I had a *Psychology Today* magazine with me, and wouldn't you know, they had a body image survey in it for their readers to fill out and mail in. S. and I looked at it together. She loved her body and I hated mine. You talk about messages being sent? I was getting them with both barrels.

First, the videotapes of the reunion frivolity were embarrassingly telltale. Pictures don't lie. Then, these two tanned and totally proud physical specimens sit next to me and we do a body image survey together. Ouch! Adding insult to injury, S. and T. munched on corn chips and candy bars. Grinning from ear to ear, S. said, "Such naughtiness can be indulged in when you work out regularly."

Okay, okay! I got the message already, but just to keep me on track, could I have a picture of them? They were more than happy to oblige me, so when we landed in the Dallas-Ft. Worth airport, they not only let me take their pictures, they even struck poses just like on TV in the middle of the concourse. I couldn't believe it. Naturally a crowd gathered, so I played press agent to get the questions rolling, then gave S. a hug and ran for my plane.

All this happened a week ago, so now I suppose you want to know if I've paid attention to all those messages. S. said it would take three months to see significant results and that I should take pictures in the same poses every month.

Then she promised I'd be hooked. We made a pact that I'd send her the slacks I was wearing on this eventful day of our meeting. Only time will tell.

§

Time to Think

When asked by a friend what I did over the Fourth of July holiday, I replied, "Oh, nothing. I was lazy and spent the weekend just thinking and writing those thoughts down in my journal."

Afterward I thought about my response. What I really said was that thinking equals *nothing*, that it is wasted time. I had not been productive in the usual sense, i.e. I had not been doing something that could be readily seen by others or that would make me money like writing an article to sell. I was amazed to hear myself utter such an inanity.

If there is anything the American of the twentieth century needs, it is time to think, time to sit quietly and contemplate his life, the world, relationships, whatever concerns him. All of us think a great deal every day, but that thinking time is mostly occupied by our need to solve problems: those on the job, in the home, with our family and friends, and in the community in which we live.

But how many of us ever find the time to take an entire day to sit or walk, quietly contemplating life with no particular problem to solve and no deadline to meet? I do it a lot, but I also find myself feeling guilty that I have not been more productive, that I have thrown a day away. And yet, when I think about this thinking time, I realize that is very productive indeed. I often reach understandings of myself or of others that greatly enhance my relationships and improve the quality of my work and my life in general.

The problem with thinking is that you can't see it and often can't readily see the results. You may feel the results, but even when you do, it is hard to convince anyone else that you have not just been lazy and are now trying to justify your laziness by saying you were thinking.

I remember as a practicing psychiatric social worker with a private practice in the evenings that untangling the knots and snarls in someone's life took a lot of time and money. The results often came far down the road. Getting started in therapy is not as hard as hanging in when the going gets slow and tough. A new wardrobe or a new car feels a lot better in the short run.

Taking time regularly to think, to let one's mind open up and wander wherever it wants to go, is like investing your time in therapy. It isn't flashy like a new car, and you can't show it off like a new wardrobe. Most people would not volunteer that they spent the weekend thinking or that they were in therapy. Both, unfortunately, connote that something is wrong, when in fact it really means that something is very right.

Taking time to think is taking time to invest in the most important person you know—yourself.

§

Arrogance as Dressed-Up Insecurity

In my capacity as an administrator, I was in the process of interviewing prospective employees. A graduate student looking for a job contacted me. Because of his class and work schedules, I made a very early-morning appointment. I was willing to make that effort on his behalf because working your way through school is tough.

The morning of his appointment, he did not show up and 30 minutes later called to say he didn't forget, he "just didn't get it together in time." Couldn't I reschedule? He couldn't come then (or at three other times I offered) as he had class in a few minutes and another job, etc.! I had made a 7:45 a.m. appointment for him just so he could make it to his 8:30 a.m. class and not be late for his job at 9:30. His tone was nonapologetic and arrogant. It implied, "of course" I could be bothered to reschedule to suit him. To hire him was to do myself a favor. What audacity!

If I were struggling to get through school and had a chance to make some very good money, I think I'd get myself "together" for a job interview, wouldn't you?

Furthermore, I don't think I'd tell my prospective employer that this, that, and the other times were just not convenient for me. When applying for a job, I believe the convenience factor is weighted on the side of the inter-viewer, not the interviewee.

Am I getting too conservative in my old age or am I just getting tired of accommodating the presumptiveness of those individuals who think the world owes them? What is it about arrogance that irritates me so much? Am I jealous? Envious?

When I want to understand something and the usual questions of "What does this mean?" don't work, I try to flip the coin over and ask the opposite question, even if it is absurd. Another way of saying this is when you see an extreme behavior in one direction, let the imaginary pendulum swing to the opposite extreme and see what you get.

Arrogance is an extreme behavior in my book. It is the extreme of self-confidence, of self-love, of security. Or is it? If my tardy student were really secure and full of confidence, what was his need for arrogance? If he is confident and secure, then so be it. If something is so, is it not so all by itself, without all the pomp and circumstance?

So what, then, is the opposite of arrogance, of this posturing and cocky attitude? Could strutting really be a cover for a faltering step? Do you crow when you really feel only capable of whispering? Do you act cocky when you really want to cry? Is the tough guy really a coward?

When I notice that I am overreacting to a person or situation and pointing an accusatory finger at someone else, I eventually calm down and say, "You know, ole girl, one finger is pointing out and three are pointing back at you. 'Methinks thou protests too much.'"

Yes, arrogance makes me mad. It is one of the least adaptive ways to handle insecurity. You don't get any sympathy from others and you are lying to yourself to boot. I think arrogance, in the other guy or in me, may only be insecurity in fancy clothing.

§

The Quick Fix

One of my more fascinating and most costly hobbies is browsing through bookstores. If I didn't have to eat and pay the mortgage, I would probably spend every penny I earn on books. One of the sections I find most fascinating is the seemingly endless supply of self-help psychology books, each promising a quick fix for whatever may ail you.

I've been thinking a lot about what people are really looking for when they buy such books. We are an action-oriented people in this country. A patient, plodding, one-step-at-a-time approach to life is not the American way. Life in the fast lane seems to be the goal of many, so it is not surprising that when trouble comes up, we look for a quick and easy solution that will not break our stride anymore than necessary.

Even those of us who are schooled in the certain knowledge that problems take time to develop, so they will take time to resolve, turn to these self-help books when pressures mount and panic threatens. I've certainly read my share of *How to...* and *I'm okay so you're okay* books. All of them have had a point or two that seemed to relate to my dilemma in some way, but none really helped all that much.

The striking thing about each of these books is that they tell the story of how the author found some solutions to his life and its problems, which may not have anything helpful to offer you and your problems.

The irony of such books is that when you buy one, you are really seeking some answers or some method to find answers for yourself, and what you get is the method and answers the author found for himself. It can be helpful to see how another person approached a problem and what he discovered, but in the end the help is limited.

Just the act of buying someone else's book is essentially saying that you do not have the information or the methods to help yourself, so you must turn to the experts, and if a book got published, the author must be an expert of some kind, right?

This need to turn outward to others, who of course, know more than you, is epidemic in this country. Some decades are worse than others, but generally speaking you can find any number of movements to join to give your life meaning and purpose and to solve your problems.

Gurus and their colonies of devotees are as readily available here as they are in India. Religions of every description and degree of extremism are everywhere. Political, economic or intellectual esoteric causes have their distinct memberships.

The militant and the passive alike, and all shades in between, can find a group with which to deposit their passions and their problems. The common denominator in all of these is the outward orientation, the turning to others for answers.

I'd like to propose my own quick-fix solution. It is the quickest fix you will ever find because you don't have to go anywhere, seek out anyone else, or deplete your resources for the cause. I'd like to call it the *Back to You Movement.* All you have to do to join is turn inward to the wonders of yourself.

§

Sowing Your Oats

When I was a young woman (I mean, younger woman), I wanted to save the world or, at the very least, help a whole lot of people. To that end, I took the education (in social work), talent and skills that I had and, like an overenthusiastic farmer, sowed my seeds in the largest field I could find with the broadest stroke of my arm. I was too young and too eager to notice that the soil was not the best and the wind was blowing. It came as a shock to me to see that so little grew from my expansive efforts, that I had done so little good.

Over the years I have learned that enthusiasm and caring are not enough. Good intentions are not enough. You have to use your head, plant your seeds of skill and knowledge in a planned way, in good soil, and on days when the wind is not blowing against you.

I have reached that wonderful crucible of midlife when you review what has and has not worked to date and you are too tired to charge once again down that road of if-I-just-try-hard-enough-it-will-work. I am at that place where I want to take the very best of my knowledge and skills and sow them in the very best soil and in a smaller field where the resulting crop will be healthy and hearty. And while the size of the harvest will not feed many, that little good I do can be used as seed grain for future good-work farmers.

Another metaphor for this image of how to do the most without wasting your resources is the pebble-in-the-pond effect. If I am the pebble and I throw that pebble into the ocean, it will be lost and the ripple effect will be overwhelmed by the waves, currents and tides. But if I throw my pebble, myself, into an exquisite pond of still water and cleanly defined shorelines, then the ripple effect will be seen, felt and heard to the opposite sides.

When you read all the books on growing up and growing older, one of the main themes is that of coming to terms with who and what you are and are not and never will be.

Mostly, these books cite the anguish of men who have to come to terms with never becoming the president of a corporation or a genuine hero of some kind or other. But women too must make peace with the limits and even failures of their careers, be they that of a wife and mother, business executive or academic professor.

For me, the reckoning is with having invested so much time and energy in trying to help others and in reality doing so little good. I wanted to be more useful to mankind. But mankind is the ocean. Now I must do what I have always done best. I must help one person at a time and let that help generate a ripple that will affect others I will never know.

I find much solace and perspective in nature. She provides so many examples of the wisdom we humans learn with so much difficulty. If only we would listen to her more. "A life of great achievement is done one day at a time, one hour at a time, one detail at a time. A great tree grows a quarter of an inch at a time...sometimes less." I wrote that in my first book, *Window to my* Soul. I wish I would take my own advice more often.

§

Manifest Destiny...

When I don't understand something, I usually sit down and write about it in hopes that the light of sudden insight will come on. What I don't understand at the moment is why do Americans move so often when moving one's residence is such an awful ordeal?

Three guesses who moved to a new house last week! I'm so traumatized by the upheaval, I can barely sleep, and I manage to find all manner of things to do to avoid unpacking. I look at the mountain of boxes and can't decide where to start, so I don't start at all.

The idea to relocate, be it across town or across the country, is usually in pursuit of the so-called American Dream, otherwise known as the bigger—better—more— syndrome.

Your family expands and you need more room. Your income expands and you want more room for all the things you can now afford. Your position in society expands and you need the proper property to reflect your improved station and to be assured everyone else knows too.

You face middle age, and financial security looms over your head, and you realize real estate is money in the retirement bank. You move to get away from certain people or situations, or you move to *find* certain people and situations. Whatever your reason, you decide the time has come.

Now the packing begins. Slowly, at first, you caress and reminisce about every object you pull from the back of that closet you haven't looked in for two years. Time slips away. The pace quickens. The urge to toss out the clutter of the past takes over like a possessing demon, and the garbage men groan while your friends who are garage sale addicts cheer. Either way, you start to clear your life and house of memorabilia and downright useful items you'll wish you'd kept a year from now. But who can think that far ahead?

Now your efforts are beginning to show. The bare walls with their telltale nail holes from treasured pictures stare back at you coldly. The wood floors echo without their companion scatter rugs. You reach in the cupboard out of habit for a familiar glass and it's not there.

As the time grows short, you're reduced to living out of a suitcase and cooking with your camping gear when you just can't manage another fast-food hamburger and fries. Your kids are declaring their intent to run away, lock themselves in the basement or be adopted by their best friend's family. They are not going to move to that yucky new house no matter what! Their trauma is worse than yours because they didn't have a say in the decision to move. They feel victimized. Familiarity, their best friend in their world of security, is being taken away from them. Aunt Jane tells them how exciting it will be to live in a big new house and she gets a scowling "no" shouted in her face for all her good intentions.

Finally, the day comes. The movers arrive, though late, and the wrenching farewell begins. Box by box, piece by piece, your life is dismantled and carried out the door by men who couldn't care less. It's a rotten job, lady.

The kids refuse to get into the car, the dog hides under the porch, the cat is in the tree, and the box with your wedding crystal is dropped. Then that last box is carried out, and you are left alone for one last walk through those empty halls. It is one of the loneliest moments in life.

Eventually you all arrive at the new house, moving van, kids, dog and cat more or less intact. In spite of your directions to put this here and that there, everything seems to end up dumped in the middle of the main room. You can't find anything you need and your one change of clothes is taking on a life of its own.

The sense of disruption is so overwhelming it is all you can do to keep yourself together and present some semblance of stability for the kids. You keep reminding yourself to be sure to yell at them as you always did for all the things they always do to be sure you're the same parent as before. The house and neighborhood may have changed but you must not. "No" must still be no in spite of the shambles of your own heart and a creeping fatigue that makes suicide more and more attractive.

Time, of course, smoothes out the wrinkles of newness and sees you put everything in its place and start to collect all the kinds of junk you just tossed out. And just as you told your husband after the difficult birth of your second child, that you'd kill him the next time he touched you, so now you swear with equal vehemence, you will never move again. You had a third child, however, and so will you probably move again. The question still remains, why?

You say it is because you'll need to, when the job changes or a better one is offered; when the family grows too large; when the neighborhood grows too small for your dreams. Do you really need to move or is your need just a great big want, and, if so, where does that want come from?

From the first ocean crossing of the Pilgrims to the Manifest Destiny of westward expansion, we Americans have been a people who have moved on in a seemingly endless search for better, bigger and more. The grass may or may not be greener over there, but how will you know if you don't go and look and even stay there awhile?

§

The Double-Edged Sword of Envy

The old people of today are the survivors of yesterday. The seniors we dismiss so easily in our youth-oriented culture have seen the coming of the car, the airplane, television, two World wars, a great depression, the coming and going of several Bohemian/hippie waves, the Big Bands, Rock n' Roll groups, and landing on the moon. Is it any wonder we see frequent fashion and behavioral crazes copying past eras? They were really interesting times in which to live. I think we're envious of our seniors and, like envy everywhere, instead of applauding them and theirs, we begrudge them all their successes that are now our daily "taken-for-granteds."

Envy is an interesting human dynamic, for it is both positive and negative. Envy is admiration, respect, longing and wishing with a great big *but* tagged on. That *but* turns those positives into negatives of jealousy and resentment.

For example, I am one of those who always travels with every possible tool and spare part imaginable. I check my oil, water, battery, hoses, gas and tires frequently. Yet I have friends who never give their cars a second thought before a trip, and they always make it without the slightest hitch. Life seems to take care of them and I am so envious! I wish I could approach life with as much abandon. It makes me mad that I can't.

My friends have a sense of security and confidence about life that seems to elude me. They believe everything will work out while I fuss and worry, trying to cover all the bases. Yes, life does work out for them because I'm out there taking care of the details for them. I wish someone would take care of my details!

Parents, too, struggle with envy of their children. They work hard to give their children all the advantages they never had as children, and yet feel resentful when all their work is not appreciated. At those moments, the war and Great Depression stories are dragged out and the kids screw up their faces as they listen one more time to how hard it was when their folks were their age. This provokes even more anger from the parents, and the downward spiral begins.

The parents are not really angry at their children, but rather at their own childhoods and the longings that still beg to be fulfilled. Remember, we give to others what we really want (or wanted) for ourselves. The mother whose own mother was a stranger to her now struggles to be her daughter's best friend. The father who never knew physical affection from his own father struggles at his own ineptness at such expressions with his son.

When the children reject their parents' overtures or seem to take them for granted, the parents feel outraged. But the children are not to be blamed. Because their parents *have* given them much of what they did not have as children, the kids do not have those aching, unmet needs. A parent can't help but feel envy once in a while. Glad they were able to give their children so much, they can still wish they had been given more as children. What their children have reminds them of what they didn't have.

I wonder about our society's lack of respect for our older citizens and whether one of the root causes for this disrespect isn't envy. Because they made it through more trials and upheavals than we, because they have more experience, because they seem to have more depth, we may feel both admiration and resentment toward them.

I often talk to elderly ranch women who lived in isolation, branded cattle, made soap, grew their own food, gave birth alone and buried their dead, all without a whimper. How I admire those women, and how I resent my own dependencies on television, the supermarket, doctors, and all the other services that remind me daily that I have very few real survival skills.

I call myself an independent woman, but in fact, I am pathetically dependent on innumerable specialists and conveniences. I envy my predecessors' achievements and gutsiness. I admire them and wish I were cut of the same timber. When I listen to their stories, I sometimes have to fight my irritation. What they have survived and achieved reminds me of all I have not.

I have no desire to repeat history or relive the past, but I do envy my ancestors. Their world forced them to define themselves as I have never had to. When I listen to them now, and see my reactions of admiration and resentment...of envy...I see myself more clearly. I see where I have come from, at least.

§

Summer Storms of Anger

Nature offers us ready and often dramatic areas in which to reflect upon our own human nature. Our recent deluge of stormy weather is a fine example. I have long held that the one human emotion most often expressed, and least often handled well, is anger.

There are studies that demonstrate that anger is the most frequently expressed emotion even when we're feeling the opposite. But you don't need a scientific study as proof of this. You need only observe yourself. Your kid runs into the street after his ball and is narrowly missed by a car. You grab him and shake him by the shoulders, all the while screaming at him. You act and sound angry when in fact you are scared out of your wits.

You receive a lovely and very expensive gift, one you have long coveted, but can only scold your spouse for jeopardizing the household budget. She hears only anger and feels crushed because you failed to say what you were really feeling, the delight of getting your heart's desire for a change.

These expressions of anger are most like the small, quick thunderstorms that are part and parcel of the summer weather scene. Though they often come at inappropriate times, spoiling a tennis game or a picnic, for the most part they don't add up to much, don't do much damage and are easily accommodated.

Then there are the ever-present grey clouds, hanging low, emitting drizzle on and off all day long and generally oppressing the atmosphere and the daily lives of everyone. Are there not people that way also? Their normal expression seems to be a frown and their entire being oozes gloomy vibrations. We nickname them "wet blankets" for they can dampen even the brightest of moods and discourage the most optimistic of spirits.

And what about those magnificent storms that can shake the earth to its core? The lightning cracks overhead, first at a distance and then progressively closer. Thunder chases the lightning in successive waves. Each wave, like those on a beach, reaches farther and deeper into your consciousness until you are covered with the roaring of the heavens.

Some people have storms of anger like these storms. They are the slow burners who have great tolerance until no more can be accommodated. The inner pressure builds until all hell breaks loose. The explosion of rage is awesome and may seem out of control to both the creator and the receiver.

Have you ever watched an infant get angry? He has magnificent storms. His entire being shakes with his rage. He not only screams at the top of his lungs but shakes from head to toe and punches the air with his tiny limbs. Because of his size, we think nothing of it. As a child grows older, these violent storms frighten him for he fears he will fall apart as readily as his doll did when he tore at it in his rage. Words, he is told, are a better way to express anger than punching out his offending sibling, friend or parent.

The trouble is, in this society we don't even allow ourselves a good full-bodied storm of words. We stammer and stutter like an underfed steam engine, spitting out only a fraction of what we feel. We rehearse for days as the storm builds inside, and then comes our chance and we blow it. Later we think of all the things we could have said, even brag to others that we *did* say all those things, which of course, we didn't.

So what happens to all that aborted anger?

It leaks out through our body, that's what happens to it. Your usually glowing complexion breaks out in angry, red pimples. Your back aches as if a knife has been stuck into it. Like the biting rain, you bite your fingernails until they bleed.

Words that threaten to vomit forth are stuffed back down your throat with unwanted food binges. You get sick in order to take yourself legitimately out of the provoking situation. Sickness gives you time out to cool off. Your arthritis flares up, preventing you from letting loose that punch you would dearly love to throw. Or you have a heart attack as your bottled-up rage implodes within, bursting your heart.

I once had a psychology teacher who lectured one day on children's temper tantrums and how to handle them. What he said was, "Temper tantrums are like summer thunderstorms. They are sudden and violent, shedding torrents of tears only to be over as quickly as they came. You can't do anything about them and they are good for the soil."

So it is with anger. When we are frightened we should say so. When we are grateful we should say so, and when we are angry we should be angry out loud and up front so the emotional skies may clear and the sun can shine again. Both are needed if earthly and human gardens are to grow and bloom into full flower.

§

What Is a Winner?

Like everyone else I know, I am glued to the TV every four years when the Olympic Games are held. At those times I find myself reflecting on the definition of winning. What is winning? What does it mean to win?

One such year, the television ads during the Olympics were almost of a single message, a kind of disclaimer about winning. That is, they all said that it wasn't winning that counted, but trying your best that was the real triumph. I think you would have a hard time convincing Mary Decker of that or any of the other current Olympic losers. I think that message of trying your best is a lovely one, but it is basically a way of making even the losers among us feel better about ourselves. I hope it works, but I have my doubts.

Do you think Romanian Ecaterina Szabo reminded herself that she was a winner as a person when Mary Lou Retton vaulted the gold medal away from her? Her face was not the image of inner peace and joy when Retton's perfect ten score flashed up on the scoreboard.

And did you see the men's volleyball team go crazy when they won? Did you see the women's volleyball team when they took the silver? Yes, it was farther than any U.S. women's volleyball team had gone before, but they *really* wanted the gold.

Did you see the two-man scull competition? The two winners were not selected for the team by the Olympic coaches, so these two fellows went to the trials on their own. You can't tell me their taste of victory wasn't laced with the honey of revenge.

And did you listen to the boxers? They didn't say, "I'm going in that ring and do my very best and I'm sure my opponent will, too. May the best man win!" No sirrreeeeee. What our boxers said was, "I'm the best, I'm gonna kill that guy," and the commentators cheered them on. "Boy, look at him go, he's going for blood now."

In other words, I don't think doing your best is winning. I think it is the consolation prize we give ourselves when we fail to grab the brass ring. I know that is not good sportsmanship, but I am asking a question here.

What then is winning?

When you look at the Olympians, you see clean-cut, all-American types, with muscled bodies, gleaming white teeth and rosy complexions. But underneath all that persona of sportsmanship is competitive steel. It is the steel that enabled them to discipline themselves day after day for years with the roar of the crowd ringing only in their inner ears.

Look again at that tiny, pint-sized gymnast, Mary Lou Retton. Did you see her face as she galloped toward the vault? It was one of the fiercest expressions I have ever seen. It was more than determination. She was out for blood, out for total victory, no ifs, ands, or buts about it.

These Olympian winners are no goody two-shoes. They are the fiercest of competitors. They are unabashed in their self-confidence and pride in themselves.

At the moment of victory, they beamed and said things like, "I knew I could do it, I was really on tonight." There is not a lot of modesty to be found, and only later, sometimes, do you hear thanks to the coaches or families that guided and supported the winner to victory.

Winning is subduing or conquering others. To the victor go the spoils, one of which is deferential treatment by others. Homage is paid, privileges and gifts given, honors bestowed. Everyone loves a winner. They do not love losers. Losers do not show up on cereal boxes.

The problem with winning, at least for me, is acknowledging the darker side of winning, the sweet taste of revenge, the bared-teeth grin of "I told you so." I don't think it is any mistake that many of the victors this year raised their hand in a clenched fist. It is a gesture of power, a gesture of supremacy, a gesture of dominance. Perhaps it is only *after* you are a winner that you can truly be a nice guy and a good sport.

§

If You Were a Millionaire

Sweepstakes mania, it's sweeping the country. Even magazines which would normally not resort to trickery are using them to entice Americans back to their rolls after austerity measures forced so many to cancel all subscriptions.

The dream of striking it rich overnight is probably a worldwide phenomenon, but it seems to me to be especially American in character since this land of immigrants has offered the promise of milk and honey for its two-hundred-plus-year history.

Almost every week, the news treats us to another huge multi-million-dollar lottery winner, and then the winner's neighbors, who are inevitably interviewed, always say how wonderful it is and, "I wish it were me." Don't we all! So, what would *you* do if you won a million or more dollars?

I know exactly what I would do. I'd pay my debts, help out a couple of special friends and then set up a stock portfolio for my old age. No, I would not buy a new car. I love my old '64 Chevy Nova wagon. I can fix it myself, usually with baling wire, my dogs call it home and no one can steal it unless they know the trick for getting it out of first gear.

I would probably stop working for others because I have a fledgling specialty printing business and I would like to write full time. I wouldn't stop working; I would just stop working for the other guy's pocketbook.

What would you do? And after you answer that, I have this question. What if everyone were a millionaire? What if we all could have anything we wanted? What would you do differently or the same with your money if impressing your neighbors would no longer be necessary? How much do we do to impress others, and how much do we truly do for ourselves?

Where would you buy a house if everyone could live where you could? What kind of new car would you choose now that gas economy is not a concern for you? Are you an ecological believer and energy conserver out of conviction or necessity?

Would you still buy your clothes at a factory outlet or are designer labels important, even though everyone else can have them, too? Would you buy season tickets to the theater, symphony or artists' series? Would you make more contributions to your church? Charities and other social service agencies wouldn't be needed, of course, because everyone would have enough money. Would your friends change?

This question of who we are and why we do as we do, whether it concerns our dress, our toys, our homes or our affiliations, was addressed in a book by Paul Fussell, entitled *CLASS, A Guide Through the American Status System.* In his sarcastic, tongue-in-cheek style, he lays bare American social stratification and answers my question.

If we were all millionaires, nothing would change. Money is the least influential factor in social class. We like to think money gives us class or style but, in fact, it does not. You can wear a mink coat and drive a Mercedes, but if you couldn't speak grammatically before you were rich, you won't afterwards. In short, Fussell says that our grammar, our tastes in such things as home decor, clothes, food, books and leisure activities, to name just a few, give us away no matter the moneyed trappings.

Therefore, even if you do win, or even earn, a million dollars, you will not change, not really. You may have more things, but you will not become more of a person, more of a humanitarian, more of a mother or father, or more of a friend than you are today.

If you become a millionaire, you will not be more loving or giving, though you can fool a lot of people with an abundance of gifts you can now afford.

You will not be more honest or dishonest than before either; you will just manifest either on a grander scale. Your tastes, whatever they are, will be more visible to more people.

And if this is all true, that we are what we are because of our accumulated experiences and not as a result of our bank balances, then why do we value money above the real riches of life: love, friendship, and self-esteem?

I think one of the sweepstakes winners said it best. "We're not going to stop working or travel around the world or do anything different than we always done. We ain't fancy folks, this will just make life a little easier, we think."

§

The Hidden Threads of Your Life

Have you ever noticed how life seems to talk to you? In those rare moments when you have the time and quiet to sit back and reflect on a particular event or interaction, you get inklings that there was really more to an event or encounter than was readily apparent.

Sometimes you sense the underlying significance of something that has happened to you, a thread with a loose end that begs to be tied off, but then the pace of your life carries you along, the moment passes, and you seldom get back to it. Still, that vague sense that there was a meaning hidden in there can bug you for days before it finally slips from your grasp.

I believe that life does talk to you—all the time, in fact. I believe that everything in life, even the most seemingly mundane or disconnected of events or interactions, has meaning, and that meaning can be enormously helpful to you if only you could hear it, see it, and understand it.

I probably spend more time reflecting upon life and my reactions to it than the average person. Many of my friends think I spend so much time thinking that, if I were normal, I would make myself sick. They are probably right.

Nevertheless, even the most pragmatic of people, living in the fast lane, with places to go and people to see, know intuitively that much in life is not as it first appears. They know that symbolism, hidden agendas, camouflaging figures of speech and unconscious motivations do exist, in themselves and in others.

Just the simple act of communicating with one's co-workers, friends and family can become quickly complicated with misunderstandings and misinterpreted intentions because these hidden meanings are missed.

Even more important than communication with others is communication with ourselves, *knowing* ourselves. Unless we first know what we want, what we feel and what we really think, how can we hope to communicate clearly with others?

I don't believe that life is happenstance or just a random series of events that are not related and have no significance. A tapestry is composed of individual threads, but they must relate to each other to create a complete design.

If all of life is related in some way, isn't it possible that the hidden meanings in life, those individual threads, have significance that make up the whole for each of us? Isn't it possible that in every event, in every encounter, in every communication that touches our lives, there is information that can help each of us travel the road of our lives better, more easily, effectively, happily?

Of course, the information I see in a particular event is not the same information you will see. This does not mean that my interpretation of an event is any less or more significant than your interpretation of the same event. They are just different, depending on the other circumstances of our lives.

Not only does life talk to you, but in that talking there is often a "thread" that repeats year in and year out. Again, using the tapestry analogy, step back and see your life in its entirety to date. Can you see a common thread that has consistently, even persistently, been there no matter the twists and turns?

What is the pattern, the design of your life? Is one obvious and one hidden? Where have you been? Where are you going? Do you want to? It's never too late to change the threads, the pattern. *You* are the weaver after all.

§

Carol L. MacAllister

The Seat of Real Power

As I sit down to write this week's column, I am drawn away by the compelling PBS National Geographic program *Four Americans in China.* A student, a reporter, a businessman and an English teacher are among the first to be a part of the recent Chinese open-door policy, and these four lived with the Chinese as no tourist has ever been allowed before. The program was a delight to watch because all four stories were full of hope and promise for a future world of understanding and cooperation.

This program was a much-needed tonic for me after spending the previous evening totally absorbed in programs marking the fortieth anniversary of the Hiroshima bombing that filled the commercial and public TV airways on August 6th.

I watched the award-winning films on Robert Oppenheimer and the victims of Hiroshima. Though not yet two years old when the bomb was dropped, I wept for the nameless thousands who died at Pearl Harbor and at Hiroshima, and during all the years in between.

What lunacy is war? What lunacy is it that drives men to enslave other men in the name of religion, moral or political rightness? How can slavery of any kind have any justification to it, any redeeming qualities or rightness? Why would anyone want to enslave another?

I suppose the obvious answer is power, but what is power? My dictionary says it's "the ability to act or perform effectively." How can a person's effectiveness be enhanced by a slave? A person is after all what he is or is not, irrespective of relationships to those around him.

My synonym finder says power is "ability, potency, strength, energy, vigor, guts" ...and so on. Will you tell me how the servitude of any other person can possibly bestow

112

these qualities? If you are incompetent, devoid of courage, natural talent or backbone, how could someone in your service change those facts? Camouflage is camouflage. A deception, cover-up, or facade need only be pulled away for the truth to be revealed.

Anything that is given from the outside can be as easily taken away and therefore is not yours to keep. Power taken from the servitude of others is only yours as long as your slaves agree to remain enslaved. When they assert themselves, you are finished.

So what then is real power? You can't find it in the dictionary or the synonym finder. It's an inner, soul-deep rightness with yourself that keeps you grounded when the tempests of group censors and social pressure whip at your back.

Real power is listening to your heart and instincts. Real power is serving others without servitude; needing others without ingratiating begging; working with others without using them; commanding others without degrading them.

Hitler didn't have it. He was nothing to begin with and nothing in the end. Anything he had in between, others gave to him in a desperate attempt to give themselves a sense of self-worth as well. Everyone lost.

Perhaps little Japan tried to compensate for its size and out-of-the-way location with territorial conquests, but it didn't work. Now that the power of their industriousness has developed from within, they have a real power that is causing giant nations to court them.

So it is with individuals. Worldliness is not the key to power. The size of one's heart is...the depth of one's soul...the breadth of one's mind.

§

For Whom the School Bell Tolls

With school right around the corner, it will not be long before the issue of declining standards of student performance will be in the news again. The nuts-and-bolts problems of teacher qualifications, adequate salaries, and the financing of up-to-date facilities are very important to be sure. But when any of us sit back and reminisce about our school years, most of us think about one, or if we were lucky, maybe two, teachers that really touched our lives so significantly that their influence is still apparent in what we do.

I've had a few such teachers in my four decades of traveling this life. The first was my father. Before I knew him, he was a classroom teacher, and by the time I came along he had entered the business world, yet he never ceased to teach.

Undoubtedly he bluffed his way through more than one of my persistent questions, but he loved history and believed you learn better about where you came from if you first touch history where it happened. To that end, our family of six toured the Eastern seaboard, visiting the major museums and historical parks.

Have you ever picked your way among the phantom dead bodies of Civil War soldiers or smelled the bread baking in the earthen ovens in their camps? I have. While my sisters and mother went to the beauty parlor, my brother, father and I relived the Battle of Gettysburg, muskets roaring in our ears.

Together we stood where George Washington stood at Valley Forge and in his Mount Vernon home. We walked the Smithsonian world until our legs screamed for rest. We even almost got to meet President Eisenhower during our

White House tour. History came alive for me because of my father's passion for it.

In high school I had an English teacher who loved the literature he taught. He may have taught Conrad's *Lord Jim* a hundred times, but when he taught it to my class we thought it was for the first time. He made me smell the sweaty, oppressive heat of the tropical jungle, and my heart beat in anxious rhythm as the story reached its climax. Because he loved his books so much and because he loved teaching, his infectious enthusiasm invaded my blood, and eventually this nonreader and nonwriter came to devour books and write volumes.

A college psychology teacher hooked me on the intricacies of the human heart in what is usually thought of as the course no professor really wants to teach: Introduction to Psychology. I was lucky. The head of the Psychology Department must have been smart enough to know that if he wanted to perpetuate his field, he had better put his wisest and most gifted teacher in his introductory classroom, for it would be from there that the majors and graduate students would eventually come.

Now that I am on the other side of the teaching/student fence, I was chagrined to hear a beloved colleague recently share his heartache over the demise of support for good teaching and the inflationary demand for esoteric publications and research grants for obscure projects. Scholarly work certainly has its place, but who will read it, who will care, if new minds are not electrified by the wonders of the world in classes like Introduction... 101?

The thing that is missing in all this talk about standards of excellence and teacher qualifications, and the thing that can probably never be determined, is how *do* you teach a teacher to love his subject right into his students' hearts?

§

Whatever Happened to the Rules?

Recently, when my name was given to a new professor at the university by a friend as someone fun to date and get to know the area with, I was a bit hesitant, but finally consented to a dinner date. As a rule I don't accept blind dates. Going into anything blind strikes me as just short of idiocy. Still, I made an exception this time because a Ph.D. in a mental health profession should mean some degree of decency and safety.

After all, the rules say if you are going to make a profession of helping others get their lives together, you are supposed to have your own act in order first. That is the assumption, but I should have known better. After 15 years in the mental health field myself, if there was one thing I learned, it was that the professionals usually need as much help as their clients, sometimes more.

As I casually shared my weekend plans with my office staff, one said, "Hmmmmm. I wonder where your date's wife is."

Wife? Wife? Who said anything about a wife? He didn't! My matchmaking friend didn't! The secretary I called to check him out with didn't! Hey! What happened to the rules? You know, the ones that pertain to marriage, to friendship, to everyday honesty, to doing things right?

Oh, Carol, you old-fashioned ninny. Everyone knows marriages these days have to bend to accommodate modern pressures of dual and not-always-compatible careers, etc. A little *drinkipoo* and *din-din* can't possibly hurt anything. After all, companionship is all he wanted, isn't it? Where's your flexibility, honey? Where's your understanding? Where's your good neighbor policy for newcomers to the valley?

Well, I will tell you where they are. They are in the rule book, the one I got as a kid growing up in those awful dumpy 1950s, which the fashion and TV worlds are now trying to resurrect. It's the book that says honesty, fidelity, and fair play come first. Singles date singles, marrieds honor their vows, and friends don't put their friends in compromising situations.

I'm a nonswinging single with zip sympathy for lonely husbands who are so new in town they don't even have a phone yet. I had to explain the rules in person, in 100-degree heat, high humidity, and on an empty stomach to boot! There are rules for breaking dates, just as there are rules for making them. Do it before he picks you up, not after.

§

How Will You Know Heaven When You Get There?

How will you know heaven when you get there? Never mind the stereotypical institutionalized versions of clouds, flowing white robes and angel wings. How will you know heaven when you arrive? What is heaven to you? What has made you pause and exclaim, "This must be what heaven is like!"

There are some who believe that the heaven you go to after you die is the one you have envisioned all your life. If so, then you are well advised to become aware of your idea of heaven now and even try to create it here on earth, to work out the rough spots.

I recently spent three days in the mountains around Cloudcroft, NM at a retreat for those of us who love to spin wool, silk, cotton and flax on modern versions of the ancient spinning wheel. How deeply soul satisfying spinning is to me, but that is another story.

The facility for this retreat was just one big metal building, so the afternoon naps and nighttime sleeps were taken at our individual campsites amongst the tall pines. I went up early so I could spend several hours of solitude with those pine trees and the whispering wind in their boughs.

This trip reminded me of the question, "How will you know heaven when you get there?" because I was experiencing a substantial amount of my version of heaven that weekend.

In my heaven, I would live in the mountains. Big, rugged mountains like those found in the Rockies. I want the scent of pine to greet me each morning and sweeten my sleep every night. I would live high up on the face of a mountain so my view would be expansive. My soul needs room to soar like an eagle. I also like being dusted by the first snow of the year and muffled by the clouds as they descend to soak the peaks and valleys in summer rain.

That my backyard would be more populated by wildlife than by fellow humans is also heavenly to me. I do want people to come and visit, but not to party. I want them to come to learn about themselves and their connectedness to all of life. The kind of people I want to visit me in my heaven are those who will step over a bug on the path and open the screen door to let a common fly out to its freedom. I do that.

I want a house made of field stones, hand-cut logs and big glass windows with no curtains. Logs and stones are the quintessence of safety and security to me. I remember seeing the great camps of the Adirondacks as a child: Kamp Kill Kare, Sagamore, and the like. To this day my memories of them wrap me in a warm blanket of mythic proportions of strength and protection. What storm could possibly blow down such a house? The glass windows would let me see those storms and the power of the universe while sheltering me from their destructive elements.

My dogs are a part of my heaven, and they get to come inside and sprawl in front of the fireplace or in the middle of the kitchen, right in everyone's way if they like.

The vegetable garden is outside the kitchen door and the root cellar harbors the canned and dried fruits of my labors after the harvest.

There is a shed with racks for the herbs and wild-flowers to dry and where skeins of wool that I have spun await my further good intentions. Half-finished knitting and crocheting projects will sit in handmade baskets that I have made with the instruction of a Santa Fe friend who is a real basket maker. I also have in this heaven of mine an easel that stands in the corner awaiting yet another attempt by me to paint something, anything that resembles nature's masterpieces just outside my door.

There is much more to my idea of heaven, and all of it so close and yet so far from my grasp. Since the slower pace of summer makes room for quiet contemplation, I urge all of you to consider this question: "How will you know heaven when you get there?" I am, of course, assuming that is where you are going.

Then, once you have an idea of what comprises heaven to you, go about creating it here on earth. Even if that is not where you end up, it will make your life on earth so much nicer. How can you lose?

§

AUTUMN

§

Saying It Like It Is

Saying it like it is. Why don't we? I'm not talking about telling people what's wrong with them. That, we all get enough of! In fact, many of us are our own worst critics. I'm talking about telling people what is right with them. Not compliments really. Compliments are more praise, tributes, homage and honors paid on occasion and in response to an unusual achievement or recognition.

No, I'm talking about telling people each day at least one little something that is good about them. It is called appreciation and we just don't seem to do it very often.

For example, when you receive bad service at a restaurant, you can register your discontent by leaving a stingy tip. But what do you do when the service is great? Do you really leave a bigger than normal tip or do you just put down the normal percentage? You may even say to your dining partner that the service is superb, but do you tell the waitress or waiter? Why not? Will your tongue fall out of your head if you do?

How many of you mothers ever remember getting a call from somebody's mother about your kid that was good news? Every mother knows that when *somebody's mother* calls, it probably means her darling child has clobbered one of his friends again. You brace for the worst. Then miracle of miracles, the voice on the other end says, "I just wanted to tell you what a nice child you have. Hello? Hello? Are you there?"

You are speechless and suddenly bathed in the warmth of human kindness, pride in your child, and gratitude for somebody's mother being so considerate that she would call and make your day. Down the road you have the chance to do the same. When the phone goes dead, you know what that mother is feeling on the other end. Doesn't it feel goooooooooooooooooooooooooooooood?

And don't forget how lonely it is at the top. That place where the buck stops is also the place where all the complaints and criticism stop as well.

Seldom do personally proffered kudos find their way up the ladder of power and responsibility. Who tells the boss he is doing a good job? Just because he makes a big salary doesn't mean he never needs to hear those sweet words of appreciation. Since he has no peer in his immediate work environment, who is there to give those precious strokes?

Subordinates may indeed appreciate him, but to say so would be out of place or could be misunderstood as apple-polishing. But I think the subordinate *should* do the stroking. I think he or she should screw up his courage and say it like it is. It can be done without being misunderstood, and even it if is, the effort is worth it. The risk is worth it.

A friend of mine told me recently how much she appreciated her son's kindergarten teacher for making his adjustment to a new school so pleasant. She told the teacher so, and then thought the principal needed to know as well.

She gathered up her courage and marched right into the principal's office. There she met an evasively protective secretary who only reluctantly fetched her boss. He opened his office door only a few inches to preview the storm he expected that was coming his way. Storms in the form of angry parents always came his way so he assumed this was just one more such visit. When my friend had finished spreading her good news, the principal was beaming, the secretary was beaming and my friend was beaming. She had made their day worth the struggle and it felt wonderful.

Then there is my veterinarian. I call him my shrink. When I am in need of some TLC, my dogs mysteriously seem to come down with some ailment. Not once has he made fun of me for this, nor does he ever get impatient with me when I overdo the protective dog-owner role. Those dogs are like kids to me and he knows every time he treats them, he is treating the "mother" as well.

He was there at 7 a.m. on a Sunday morning to save my Doberman Pincher from near death, and he was there, crying with me, when we had to put my cancer-ridden Lab down. I'd rather pay his bill than buy groceries, and his staff is every bit as caring as he is. I'm ashamed to say, until I was conceptualizing this column, I hadn't taken the time to tell them all how much I appreciated them.

Finally, when I did tell them, I felt strangely shy and embarrassed. Why, I wondered? Why am I afraid to reach out and touch my fellow man with the tenderness of kind words? Why does such kindness make me feel vulnerable? Am I giving them the appreciation I wish others would give to me? Am I afraid my own hunger for appreciation will show when I offer it to others?

There isn't any good reason for my hesitation, but it is there, nonetheless. Maybe I need to be more courageous. Maybe I just need to practice. Yes, that's it. I need to practice. Join me, won't you?

§

Worthy Adversaries

Everyone at sometime in his life, if not all the time, has a person or situation that causes him considerable, even crippling, worry, aggravation, consternation and fits of rage. When handled badly, not handled at all, or kept inside to smolder, the sufferer can develop ulcers, migraines, nervous irritability and any number of other maladies that generally make his life miserable and contaminate the lives of those around them.

It seems to me you can view these people or situations negatively as crosses to bear or as tests to be endured, or you can view them as worthy adversaries.

Intrinsic in this concept of worthy adversaries is seeing blessings hidden in even the darkest cloud. I know this is beginning to sound Pollyannaish, but it is not.

I believe people make their own realities. If you view the world as generally a bad place where you must spend the majority of your energy guarding against those who would cheat, rob, or otherwise do you injustice, then that is pretty much what you get.

If, however, you see the world as more or less a good place where you need to be realistically cautious but not paranoid and where if you give goodness you will get goodness back, then you will experience the same positives coming toward you that you project outward. Is this not the basic theme of the timeless Dickens story, "A Christmas Carol?" Scrooge gave little and received little. He hated and was hated. He was loaded with money and bereft of the wealth of love and friendship.

I see the miserable people in my life acting that way because they feel miserable, unhappy and are more often than not filled to overflowing with anger. Their misery by comparison shows me just how happy I am even on my greyer days. Everything is relative.

Then again, if I am in a relationship that has turned sour, I am driven to get out, which makes me dig down deep to find the courage to say, "Good-bye, I'm leaving, this is bad for me."

People who abuse me force me to defend myself better.

People who are rude challenge me not to be rude back. Good manners do work, even with irritable people.

People who are stingy make me more generous. After all, you can't take it with you.

Now I am starting to sound like Mary Poppins but, you know, she was right! A spoon full of sugar does make the medicine go down, and life can be bitter medicine at times.

I know people (and I am one) who when they were laid off from their jobs found it to actually be a blessing. It forced them to find resources, humility and tenacity in themselves they didn't know they had.

Entire new careers have been started this way. They learned new skills and made new friends, all of which would have been passed by if they had not been forced to *punt*, if you will. Necessity is the mother of invention; therefore, if you can see your worthy adversaries as people or situations that are forcing you to change, stretch, and find new facets to yourself, then you can say good-bye to ulcers, heart attacks and Tums.

It is tough to be a positive soul in a world that, it seems, would rather grind you to a pulp. It's easy to disparage others, to criticize, or blame the other guy, the masses or the government for your misery, but in fact you are the author of your own fate.

When you find a situation in your life less and less tolerable, pause in the middle of your lamentations and consider what it is doing *for* you. Maybe your present misery is helping you focus on where you really want to go in the future. Maybe it is helping you to develop creative aspects of yourself hitherto denied.

There is a flip side to every coin; it need only be turned over. The dawn does follow the dark of night, but you have to be up to see the sunrise. This may require the breaking of some old patterns and opening your eyes to seeing things from a slightly different angle. If you think I'm going to O.D. on clichés, just remember they became everyday tidbits of wisdom because they have the ring of truth. We just don't pay enough attention to them.

Adversaries by definition are opponents or the enemy. They do not have to defeat you, however, even when they appear to have won. If, in the wake of the battle, they have made you more worthy, then it is you who has won the war.

§

Now It's My Turn

A mother stands over her precocious 2-year-old admonishing him to share his toy with a visiting friend. "No!" he replies. "It's mine, I want."

From the mouth of babes come the truths of the world, or so the sages tell us, and I'm with the sages. It is hard to share even when you become a thoroughly civilized adult, having learned all the appropriate reasons and rewards for sharing with others.

Any parent will tell you that as they struggle to teach their child the importance of sharing, they themselves become the masters of compromise. Billy won't share his train with Jimmy, so a compromise is struck and Billy gets to play with half of it and Jimmy gets the other half. Now any child knows a train without an engine or without a caboose is no train at all, so both end up crying and deserting the dismembered train for something else.

And so it goes. From the simplest of conflicts to the most complex in the business world, deals are created and compromises hammered out so no one gets what they really want, yet no one goes away empty-handed. When negotiating for a job, a raise or a position of power, finding that delicate balance is the job of the arbitrator, or even of oneself. It is what makes the world function.

But wouldn't you like to get exactly what you want once in a while? Aren't you sick to death of sharing and compromising so that nowhere and at no time do you ever feel really satisfied deep down?

Here is an idea for you, a compromise, if you will.

Let's take a typical domestic scene. The husband has worked all day, had lunch out with his colleagues and now wants nothing more than to stay home, have a nice dinner and read his newspaper. The wife has worked all day, either in a job outside the home or doing her jobs inside the home. She wants nothing more than to be waited on in a restaurant so she can finally relax and end her working day as well. Both are tired. Neither wants to do any more work for that day, including getting dinner and cleaning it up.

The couple expresses their desires. Neither wants what the other wants, so they strike a compromise. They order out for pizza. The husband has to go out one more time to get it, and the wife gets the job of cleaning up the mess. In the end, neither gets the caring attention they want and need.

Why not take turns? The husband consents to going out for dinner to give his wife what it is she needs and wants, and the next time this comes up, she gives him what he wants.

It seems to me that if you agree to give each other turns, then when you give in to the other, there is no resentment. It isn't a question of one partner giving in to the dominance of the other. Nor is one being the martyr who then complains silently through little hostile gestures, like her burning the dinner or his forgetting his billfold in the restaurant.

When you take turns, there need not be resentment or sacrifice. If both know that in due time they will get their turn, then the giving can be full-hearted and unabridged, and that alone can be very satisfying.

Since most people's workaday worlds offer them little control, and the variety of people and situations require an endless succession of compromises, it seems to me that in one's personal life one should make room for getting those needs and desires for the "I wants" satisfied.

And I think children of all ages need to be included in this kind of giving turns also.

Two-year-olds aren't the only people who want what they want when they want it. They are just less civilized about telling us.

When people hear a child scream his protest at sharing, most see a brat in the making. I see a vestige of my younger self and I hear a tiny voice buried deep within under multiple layers of socialization struggling to break free.

§

You Get What You Pay For

It strikes me that everything is life is related. With a little imagination, parallels and analogies can be drawn that help to clarify some of the more troubling or hard-to-understand problems we all face.

Relationships, whether personal loves, friendships, work-based or only casual encounters, concern everyone and occupy the majority of most people's time. Wherever you go, if you tune in to conversations around you, you will hear people debating what went wrong or what went right in any particular liaison.

I think of relationships much like the houses of the *Three Little Pigs.* The house of straw is built easily, and costs very little to construct. Since straw is lightweight, there is no need for a strong solid foundation to be laid. There are relationships like this straw house, too. Built overnight, based on sex, having to work together, or working just for a paycheck, these relationships stand up just fine in good times. But in times of trouble, the straw collapses if hit by the slightest wind of provocation.

The wood house is an improvement on the straw one, though it costs more in dollars and time and takes longer to build. People who share one or two things in common and base their friendship on these have relationships like this wood house. They are agreeable in fair weather and can withstand mild storms, but given a good nor'easter type blow, they crumble like matchsticks.

Then there are those relationships built like a brick or adobe house. Solid like a fortress, they are very expensive in time, effort, and dollars to build. The foundation must be strong, built on mutual respect, affection and many shared interests.

In fair weather, this house is cool and tranquil. In the foulest of gales, it stands strong, impervious to the tempest beating at its walls. The big bad wolf can come time and again, but the house will stand, cemented by loyalty born of the daily effort it took to build the relationship over the years.

Think of the marriages, friendships, working relationships you know of that were like the straw house. They crumbled easily, of course, vulnerable to the first strong wind that came along, and storms come to marriages, friends and jobs quite frequently.

Then there are those like the wood house. They stand up longer, but become weaker and weaker with each battering. Over time, even repairs won't save them. These relationships just die a slower death than the ones made of straw. They looked so good in the beginning, but they do not wear well over time or weather the tests of life.

But the brick houses endure and even mellow over time. With repeated attention to the surface injuries caused by the challenges life inflicts, these houses, relationships or jobs have a timeless quality to them. They develop their own patina, their own character, and become unique.

I've had and do have relationships and jobs like all three of these kinds of houses.

My first job out of graduate school lasted ten years. Over that time, lifelong friendships were forged, personal histories recorded and celebrated, and the lessons of life engraved on the hearts of those who were there. I've had jobs that looked good but just broke down after a while, and jobs that blew away overnight.

My love affairs seem to fall into the same categories. Those based on pure chemistry are long gone. Those that developed at a specific time and place (i.e. college or a work place) died more slowly, but die they did.

And then there are those that, while no longer love affairs in the conventional sense, have become friendships of affection and respect that will last for all time. The love I have for each of these people, and theirs for me, does not need daily contact to keep it alive. Nor does it exclude other people or even other loves from coming into our lives. But the love we first felt has grown and mellowed, and allows us to touch without possessing, to talk without pretense, to give without strings attached.

I have often thought that one of the primary qualifications of a spouse or friend or even an employer would be the presence of long-term and enduring loves, friends and colleagues in their lives. It would be proof that this person is cherished and respected, and hence my caring and respect would be well placed and may be returned in kind.

Some people cannot tolerate sharing their love or friend or colleague with others. They believe, mistakenly, that to share is to dilute and to divide the rewards, when in fact to share is to multiply and increase the bounty.

But then to share yourself and to share those we love with others takes time and effort, and after all, as it is with houses, so it is with people. You get what you pay for.

§

The Paradox of Insomnia

Early to bed, early to rise, makes a man (or woman) healthy, wealthy, and wise.

If you add to this formula eight hours of sleep, you have the formula by which I fuel my daily activities. I'm like a kid. I need a good night's sleep and when I don't get it, I'm crabby, short tempered, inefficient, and, if I had my druthers, would throw a tantrum or two.

Lately I've been without several nights of sleep. After eliminating the usually named culprits, spicy food, late coffee, pressure at work and love-life traumas, I was left with the mystery of insomnia, the plague of millions.

It was easy to see what my lack of sleep was doing to me. I looked like death warmed over, my back was rigid with superimposed tension to hide my fatigue, my manners had faded to perfunctory acknowledgments, and my smile had vanished. Yet knowing all this did not help me understand why I was not able to sleep night after night.

One of my standard rules when confronted with a mysterious situation or a frustrating pattern is to flip the coin over, turn the sock inside out and ask the absurd. If I know what this stupid insomnia was doing to me, against me, then, as absurd as it sounds, I ask, "What could it be doing for me?" By knowing what my insomnia was doing *to* me, I hadn't discovered a thing. Perhaps the answer lay in the opposite direction. Could my wakefulness be serving me in some way?

I decided to pursue this tack further. What did I have to lose—more sleep? I would accept the idea that my insomnia was helping me in some way, but how? I decided to look at what I was doing during those wee hours of the morning when I should have been sleeping. Literally, what was I doing?

To my surprise, I discovered that I was thinking. No, I was not obsessively worrying about something, nor was I reviewing past or rehearsing future encounters with others. I was not being kept awake by worries. I was thinking, very productively, very creatively about new writing, about business projects, about burgeoning relationships, and about my immediate and distant future. The fact was, in the midst of my awful insomnia, I was doing some very exciting planning.

But then the question became, "Why do I need to be doing this in the middle of the night?" It was the kind of thinking I usually do in the afternoons and evenings. Then it dawned on me that I had been deprived of that usual thinking time lately because of deadlines at work. These were then compounded by my recent decision to join the health club fitness craze. Working out each day takes time, lots of it, and it was taking my thinking time away from me.

My younger, Minneapolis-based sister, who is a runner, was asked by our mother at a recent family reunion, "Do you *have* to run every day?" as she looked at her rain-soaked child packing her sore heel in ice. My sister's response was, "Do you have to breathe?"

What appears to be a luxury to some is a necessity to others. An integral part of my sister's existence is her running. An integral part of my existence is time to think. If

I don't get my daily dose during my waking hours, I will take it during my sleeping hours by not sleeping.

So there it was. As irritable and exhausted as my insomnia had made me, it had also given me something I obviously valued more than rest and feeling good physically. It gave me time to think about my life.

Think yourself about what in your life is apparently hurting or hindering you and then ask boldly, plainly, literally—what could it be doing *for* you? It works for me. I've been sleeping like a baby ever since writing this column and cutting back my gym workout time.

§

Bring Back Old-Fashioned Courting

After listening to a friend cry her way through the aftermath of yet another torrid love affair wrecked on the rocky shores of sex before the sails of friendship had even been hoisted, she asked me what it was I wanted in a dating situation.

Her style of open, all out, sex-first-talk-later relating was obviously very modern and very disastrous. So what was my answer to the modern woman's dilemma of too-easy intimacy?

"I'd like to see old-fashioned courting make a comeback," I said, after giving her question a lot of consideration.

Courting means that you ask to visit a lady at her home. Courting means when you go visiting you do so with a small bouquet of flowers or other token of affection in hand.

Courting means, you go to meet each other's parents or friends, to pass muster, so to speak, and declare one's intentions as honorable and genuine.

Courting means to take time, lots of it if necessary, to get to know each other by talking, and talking, and talking some more.

Courting means you first gaze into each other's eyes before holding hands. Holding hands precedes a kiss. The peck on the cheek precedes a peck on the lips and the peck on the lips then heralds the long kiss. I'm a big fan of the long kiss. I think it's a great place to linger or even camp out for a while before thinking about anything more serious.

The only modern touch I would add to old-fashioned courting is I'd have the woman give flowers and candy and write love notes as often as the man. I've never met a man yet who didn't love to get a bouquet of flowers, though he might not admit it. I once sent my brother a dozen long-stemmed red roses for his birthday and so did his girlfriend! He beamed as he reported he was the envy of every salesman who walked into his office for weeks thereafter.

Courting would revive the flower, candy, and love note business, to say nothing for candlelight dinners. So you see it would make economic sense as well as romantic sense. And courting would bring boy*friends* and girl*friends* back in to fashion. That is, friendships between men and women would become the building blocks for the house of love that might be built later on. That foundation would be strong because each block would have been laid down one at a time and in the proper order.

The sexual revolution in the sixties and seventies put the cart before the horse. The novelty was exciting at first, but horses pull, they don't push, so the cart really couldn't go anywhere unless it rolled out of control. Old-fashioned courting would put the horse back in his pulling harness and put the cart back on the road of love and romance.

§

Reunions: A Trip Back in Time

Summer is a time for family vacations, adventures or whatever activities you may choose to give you time out from your normal day-to-day life. If you are forty-something, summers can also be a time for high school reunions. I have just returned from my thirtieth high school reunion, and I confess to still being in a time warp. It doesn't help that as I write this, *American Graffiti* is on TV with Richard Dreyfus looking so wet behind the ears I can hardly believe he is of my era.

I returned to the rolling hills of upstate New York to visit my brother and mother, and to visit my past as well. Each day I drove old familiar roads where I passed the same white clapboard farmhouses that were old when I was just a kid riding the yellow school bus that took us to school each morning. They had not changed a bit. Those old roads took me around bends, across creeks and through woods that looked exactly as they had thirty years ago when I last saw them. Urban sprawl had not found this sleepy corner of rural New York State.

I visited a local county park, the site of an eighteenth-century flour mill. I walked in the woods alone and shivered with a visceral memory of so many walks like that one so many years before. The woods were where I sought solace for my soul even as a teen.

I visited the city house in which I was born and the country house where I was raised. It is perched high on a hill above the valley town where I attended school. There are a few new buildings in town, and a few old ones have burned down, but for the most part all is exactly as I left it when I graduated and put a tentative foot out into the bigger world. The white steepled church where I taught Sunday school is still there, and so is the town pub right across the street. They have coexisted that way since the beginning, I guess.

And there was my old school, still as implacable as ever; red-bricked, arched leaded glass windows, wainscoted walls, and stained glass windows in the door to each classroom. One of my classmates, who had moved away but returned to raise his family in this small, little changed rendition of Americana, arranged for a yellow school bus to pick up the class at the park where we were picnicking and delivered us, as in the old days, to the steps of the school, where a very modern and very indulgent vice principal gave us a tour of the old school.

Like little kids again, we raced from room to room, remembering which teacher had which room and then, all talking at once, sharing a rush of memories about that teacher, that class, that subject and that year. Everyone seemed to remember much more than I did, but that did not lessen the flood of feelings that washed over me with each hall we walked down.

We had all met at the town park, which is where as grade-schoolers we went at the end of each school year for our annual school/class picnic. I can feel those picnics to this day and how special they were to me. Here we were again, having a clam bake with all the fixin's and ignoring the threat of rain just like we always did. (Rain never stops folks who live in rainy country. It is only we who live with sun most of the year that get waylaid by a little bad weather now and then.) It did rain, too, very hard, but we all just moved closer together under our shelter and kept talking and talking.

I took my graduation yearbook and it was a good thing, too. I didn't recognize anyone at first! They all said I hadn't changed at all, but they surely had; though once I found their senior picture and compared it to the forty-something version, the similarities were clear.

A few of my old school chums I did recognize immediately. My very first real boyfriend I knew instantly. He could still make my heart skip a beat. Our first date in the sixth grade was to a movie, chaperoned by his mother.

Chaperoned! Do kids these days even know that word? He was more gorgeous than ever, and oddly enough, his younger brother lives near me in New Mexico, just down the road a few hundred miles, an afternoon's jaunt by New Mexico standards.

We've all promised to write, but of course will not. I've made that promise with many old friends over the years, friends from my post-college days and former job colleagues, but we never have written and probably never will.

I returned to New Mexico via my younger sister's home in Minnesota and a side trip to Madison, Wisconsin, to visit friends not seen in years. Unlike my high school friends, these latter-day friends seemed exactly as they had been twelve years ago.

The passage of time and my memory of those bygone years are very strange to me. I don't live in the past, nor do I long for it, and yet it is strangely comforting to have a past with others who knew me when I didn't really know myself.

§

Rise and Fall of Petty Tyrants

A letter from a friend from yesteryear came last week, and it brought back a flood of memories of the times and work we had shared years ago.

Both of us were psychiatric social workers in a large training medical center. One of the duties that fell to us, because the psychiatric residents didn't want to mess with it, was to consult with the medical staffs of three critical care units; the burn treatment unit, the kidney dialysis unit, and the pediatric cancer unit.

The job really was to provide a forum for the nursing staffs to discuss their patients and what was happening to staff members as a result of caring for patients who could die on them at any moment.

It was the best job I ever had and the most rewarding, though my heart and soul were exercised to exhaustion almost weekly. Still I knew, and those nurses knew, they were doing *real* work and that what they were doing really counted.

The thing about working with the terminally ill is that all the superfluous junk that we clog up our lives with falls away, and you are forced to confront raw emotion and the bottom-line questions of life.

Human limitations and those of modern medicine are faced and accepted, though often through a veil of frustration and tears. The sick children comfort the adults, displaying courage and wisdom beyond their years. People who were afraid to touch physically now reach out and cling to each other.

The lies of "everything will be okay" are dropped and long-hidden secrets shared. The final farewells are spoken, and sometimes it is only the nurse who is there at the end to say good-bye and wish them well on their next journey.

This work took its toll on the nurses. It was excruciatingly difficult for them to walk the tightrope between maintaining the professional objectivity needed to execute medical procedures and giving patients the love and warmth that is as critical to healing as any medicine. Our weekly sessions helped the nurses keep this balance.

In addition to the patients, we also discussed the doctors and how some seemed to make the nurses' job easier and some made it harder. Inevitably, there was always one who would earn the nickname of Simon Legree.

One doctor in particular was a petty tyrant with delusions of grandeur that far exceeded his native intelligence, learned skills to date and personal aura. In short, he didn't have what it took to be arrogant and get away with it. He was loud and had bad breath. He never made requests. He gave orders. He was condescending when he gave instructions to the nurses and when he talked to the patients. His temper was explosive and unpredictable. In staff meetings he was known to throw pencils and slam the desk with his fists. Today he wanted things done this way and tomorrow he would reverse himself, but never acknowledge his reversal. Of course he never made mistakes. Dictators don't make mistakes, didn't you know?

The nurses hated him, the patients feared him and, as a result, the care of the patients suffered. Because the patients were afraid, they would not tell him everything that they felt or worried about. Because the nurses hated him, they would unconsciously sabotage him by not doing, or half doing, what he told them.

The patients would complain to the nurses and the nurses wanted to join them in their commiserations but couldn't if they were to adhere to their professional code of conduct. It fell to the nurses to ferret out any information critical to the care of the patient he had withheld from the doctor.

Informing the doctor often met with a verbal assault, but so it went, for the patient's sake, because *Simon* never caught the connection between why the nurses knew things about his patients he should have known. Self-reflection was not one of his skills or inclinations. It never is with any petty tyrant, and unfortunately they abound in our world and come in all forms and walks of life.

Parents torment their emotionally dependent children with threats of abandonment; teachers bully their captured charges; husbands abuse their economically dependent wives; bosses exploit their financially dependent employees;

and professionals attack and humiliate their younger colleagues. These tyrants exercise their power over the pettiest of issues in their tiny domains of the home, class-room, office or staff meeting.

All too often, it is only the specter of death that topples the petty tyrant's paper throne. So it was for the *Simon Legree* my friend and I once had to work with. In his hospital bed on the cancer ward, surrounded but not visited by the medical staff he once bullied so arrogantly, he died alone. Tyrants, even the petty ones, always do.

§

Loose as a Goose

Don't you just hate people who are loose as a goose and feel at home no matter where they are? I do! I can't do it and it makes me so envious, I could spit.

I'm one of those souls who is so organized that a magazine could do an article on time management with me as an example. Every evening I make a list of the next day's tasks and then prioritize them according to importance and/or at which point in the day achieving that task can be most efficiently completed.

Only one trip a day is made for errands, and those are done along a route so I don't waste time and gas backtracking or retracing miles already traveled. A list on the dash helps to keep me from forgetting any stops. My morning walk with the dogs is at first light and the daily swim is just before dinner to give me a second wind for the evening chores.

Since I am self-employed and work at home at this point, a checklist of daily goals helps keep me from goofing off or frittering away time. Even my social life is scheduled. Dinner with M.A. on Tuesday, lunch with D.C. on Wednesday, class Wednesday night, and so on. I even have my dental cleaning and haircuts scheduled twelve months in advance!

I get a great deal accomplished and feel justifiably smug about it. After all, am I not living up to the American dream of the efficient Protestant work ethic? Just let me get my hands on one of those *loose gooses* and I can fix up their lives in nothing flat, with one notable exception.

I have known a man for twenty years who is absolutely unflappable. In spite of our long friendship and my concerted efforts to organize him, he has remained as loose and easygoing as he ever was. In fact, he is more so. I mean it is positively maddening.

One of our favorite activities was to take long drives in the country. I'd get ready by packing an elaborate picnic and, mind you, I never forgot the corkscrew or napkins, the blanket or plastic bags for trash. To this day friends love to camp with me because I bring everything.

By eight in the morning I was packed and ready to go, complete with a list of all the antique shops I wanted to stop at along the way and a grocery list in case we passed some fruit and vegetable stands en route.

Mr. Calm, on the other hand, took a leisurely breakfast and would tell me not to worry if the gas tank was not full or the oil and water up to date. "Relax, ole girl," he'd say, with the most patient and rock-quiet calm. Maddening! He just took everything in stride, even my superwoman efficiency.

One day I finally threw a tantrum. Cheeks flushed and hands flapping, I stomped around protesting, "How do you think anything gets done around here? Me, because of me, that's how. If I don't organize everything, nothing would happen. Well, I quit. Q U I T, Quit! Do you hear me? If you want a picnic, fix it yourself. I'm not going to organize one more activity!"

"Okay," he said and smiled that infuriating smile.

"Humph," I snorted and strutted off, mumbling to myself. I'll get my revenge the next time we go off on a jaunt and he wants this, that or the other thing, and I won't have it along. And I will not take one step to go get gas when he runs out, either. It will serve him right.

Well, guess what happened the next time we ventured out? Nothing! Not a dadgum thing. I couldn't believe it. We took off on an all-day excursion and we didn't go hungry, die of thirst or run out of gas. It rained, but we didn't get wet or cold, though I left the umbrella and extra sweaters at home.

We saw lots of shops and local craft fairs though I had no must see list along. In spite of myself, I had a wonderful time and got a taste, well no, maybe a whiff, of what it must be like to be as *loose as a goose.*

I'm such a hopeless case I still make daily and weekly lists, but at least now I schedule in what I call my loose-goose times. One day a week I let life happen to me. It's the most delicious day of the week. I'm even considering expanding it to two days—that is, if I can find time in my appointment book.

They say there are lessons to be learned each day of the year. Some lessons are important and some are not so important. That the world doesn't need my organizational skills was one of the most important lessons I have ever learned. Why don't I remember it more often?

§

Body Language

Periodically on the morning talk shows another author of yet another book on body language is interviewed. As the author analyzes what crossing your legs means, and what fingers around the mouth signifies, the interviewer inevitably starts to squirm, suddenly self-conscious about the hidden messages he or she may be sending out.

It's fun and interesting and all too true. If we would only listen with our eyes, our bodies and everyone else's could speak volumes.

But body language can be carried farther than just the parlor game cues to sexual interest or white lies. Our bodies really can tell us what's bugging us well before we are consciously aware of it. The trick is to decode the language.

Actually, it isn't all that hard. In fact, our bodies leak our feelings, conflicts, or approaching changes quite literally. Our language, the terms and phrases we use in casual conversation, describe the body language which is leaking the soul's struggles.

For example, let's take a look at the all-time winner for physical and psychosomatic complaints—chronic back pain. Let's face it; Doan's Pills have survived all these years because back pain is common to almost everyone. The language we use about the back is the giveaway for analyzing its psychological root.

He's a pain in the neck or a pain in the butt or somewhere in between.

He stabbed me in the back!

I broke my back for them.

I've bent over backward to make this marriage work.

I turned my back on them in disgust.

He backed down or out of a situation to save face.

Cowards show their backs.

He had backbone and stood up for what he believed

She held herself back, struggling for control.

Just consider for a moment who or what in your life fits any, some or all of these phrases. Are you presently struggling with feeling cheated or unappreciated to the point that you are leaking your resentment behind your back? For myself, I get back pain when I'm angry at being stabbed in the back by someone I thought was a friend, or when a current situation brings back memories of former such insults.

Let's take another example of a common physical complaint, arthritis. Yes, I know there is a physical breakdown in the joints and I know there does seem to be a hereditary connection for why some people get it and others don't. However, just consider the possibility of a psychological basis for this particular physical malady.

What happens when you are arthritic? You are not flexible, loose, spontaneous, or freewheeling. You are restricted, rigid, unable to bend, slowed down, unable to move quickly or reactively or spontaneously. You are not free to come and go as you please, and others must cater to you, to lesser or greater degrees. Perhaps arthritis is only a physical consequence of old age, *but perhaps* a lifetime of rigidity and inflexibility, especially intellectually or emotionally, can also explain crippling physical arthritis. It's at least something to think about.

A couple of months ago, I developed an arthritic hip, and after hearing me complain once too often, a very thoughtful friend asked when it hurt the most. My response was that it only hurt when I had to stand up. In short, she observed, it hurt only when I had to stand on my own two feet.

At the time, I was planning to go into business for myself. It was scary, but I was determined. That insight released my body from having to express my anxieties. Then my legs began to ache. I was aching to get going on my new life.

How about muscle pains, bum shoulders, sore knuckles? Is there someone in your life you would like to punch out? Consider the lowly eye twitch. If the eyes are the windows to the soul, then we close our eyes to avoid seeing the truth and to avoid giving our true feelings away. If you were to put that twitch into slow motion, you would see your eye trying to close.

Do you suffer from chronic indigestion? What or who in your life makes you sick, or is it you? Are you being a "yellow belly" where you should be courageously confronting a dilemma?

The point is: your body talks to you and can be a real ally in helping you figure out your physical pain and how it may be directly connected to the emotional challenges of your life, present or long repressed.

Furthermore, if you will listen to your language as you describe your physical pain, your own spontaneous choice of words will provide a key piece to the puzzle of how body, mind and soul all fit together and affect each other. After all, a *punishing* headache may be exactly the retribution you think you deserve for unacceptable thoughts, wishes or deeds. So look to yourself first for the cause and the cure before you reach for the aspirin bottle or call the doctor.

§

What Makes People Impressive

I recently visited Phoenix on a business trip to promote my handmade stationery and notes. As I visited the exclusive domains of the wealthy and famous, of which

Phoenix, Scottsdale and Paradise Hills have many, I was aware of an encroaching sense of intimidation.

The galleries and resort gift shops were expensive and doing a booming business. The proprietors were as tanned and elegantly clad as their clients. In Scottsdale, you don't have customers. That would be too plebeian. One has *clients*, and even *patrons* for the repeat spender.

There were no old cars. Fortunately, I flew and didn't take my '63 Chevy. Caddies, BMWs, Lincolns and Jaguars seem to be the most popular forms of motorized travel. I even parked next to a fancy motorcar, all leather interior, with a supersonic-jet-type dashboard (please pronounce with a proper British accent), and a "Principale de Monte Carlo" license plate.

It clearly had been flown over for the American tour of its owner, who probably did not want to be bothered with the hassles of renting an inferior American auto. I really wanted to wait until the human component of that motorcar appeared instead of casing the exclusive shops of La Borgata for likely retail settings for my art work. However, responsibility overcame my curiosity. When I reappeared from the inner courtyards of exclusivity, the car was gone.

It's just as well. I wouldn't have liked being seen in my shorts with legs that needed tanning and my less-than-chic, but oh so comfortable, Birkenstock sandals. Not exactly the outfit with which to impress a prince.

By the time we visited the town of Carefree, the retirement playground of the well-to-do, and the Arizona Biltmore, where the room prices and the menu prices are seldom printed, I was thoroughly intimidated and wondering why.

Everyone puts their pants on one leg at a time. The rudiments of bodily functions and needs are not altered in any way by wealth or fame. Human happiness still depends on the same basic laws of love, intimacy, appreciation and a sense of purpose. Riches won't bring you love. Maybe lots of parasitic flatters, but not love. So why was I intimidated?

Because, I think, I was insecure about myself and about my art. My self-doubts gave others credit and attributes they may or may not have deserved. After all, there is no correlation between personal integrity and wealth. In fact, some would argue an inverse correlation exists.

The Have-Nots especially feel no rich man ever came by his wealth honestly. I wouldn't go that far because I know poor people who cheat to get something for nothing or at least less, and I know middle income people who do the same. I don't know very many really rich people, so how can I judge?

What I do know, however, is that the people I am truly impressed by are those who stand tall, secure in who and what they are, regardless of their external trappings. They like themselves.

I also know people who have a big city coiffure, dress in the latest preppie styles, and have not a phony hair on their heads. I stood among such crisp personas last summer at my brother's wedding, draped in my brightest purple Mexican dress, feeling terribly conspicuous. I was incredulous when a real preppie, clad in altogether proper beige and navy, admired my freedom to wear such bright colors! I may have felt like apologizing, but I didn't need to. I had been perceived as more confident than I felt because I had dared to stand out. Someone else's insecurity was crediting me with confidence I didn't actually feel at the time.

I was doing the same in Phoenix, to nameless, faceless hundreds just because they drive fancier cars than I do, and because their houses are bigger and more expensive looking than mine, a humble little solar, mud and log affair.

When I had a chance to look at all this, it came to me that the people I feel are truly impressive are the people who do not make me feel inferior in spite of their obvious superiority in some areas. Since I am the only one who can feel inferior, then I guess everyone will be impressive in some way, once I am secure about myself.

§

A Ten-Year-Old Gentle...man

Ladies and gentlemen, the youth of America is not going to wrack and ruin, at least not all of it. A friend of a friend of mine in Phoenix, whose age can only be guessed at since she is fit, tanned and energetic, is the grandmother of this ten-year-old. Her name is Shirley; his is Doug. Since we were to spend all day Saturday together exploring ancient Indian ruins, Shirley introduced my friend and me by our first names.

However, she noted that this was an exception to the normal rule they operated by. Children do not call their elders by their first names in this family's modis operandi. I liked that. It was how I was taught. Children are not equal to adults and should not be misled into thinking they are.

Doug, for his part, knew that this first-name business was an exception and struggled with it all day. Sweet!

Our foursome headed north of Phoenix, reading a roadside geology and history primer all the way. What else do you do with three schoolteachers in one car?

It was two hours before we saw our first Indian ruins, and Doug didn't squirm, complain, or ask to go potty or to stop for food. He said please and thank you at appropriate places and didn't need coaching to remember his manners, as even some adults I know do. He loved Montezuma Castle, thought Montezuma's Well "neat-oh," and Tuzigoot "nifty."

When the adults voted for classical music on the radio, he declared his interest in playing the cello if he could find room to schedule lessons in between his break dancing practice, gymnastics and baseball.

He used words like fantastic and significant, and told me in no uncertain terms that he couldn't tell me what he would be when he grew up because he hadn't lived long enough to know all the choices he had. "After all," he said, "I'm not even in high school yet. I am only ten, you know."

I didn't talk like that when I was ten years old. I did know what I wanted to be. First a cowgirl, and then a nurse, a teacher and an airline stewardess! We were so sure back then. Kids today are sure of nothing and it doesn't seem to bother them one bit. At least Doug found it to his advantage to leave all his options open.

We were on the road ten full hours and he ate what was packed in the picnic basket, even declaring the soda we brought along to be his current favorite! Sweet kid!

When his grandmother corrected his grammar, he took it in stride. When I couldn't resist giving him a hug, he let me, and when the grownups snoozed on the ride home in the dark, he talked quietly with the driver.

When I told Doug what a nice young man I thought he was and what a good traveling companion, he said thank you without embarrassment, discomfort or bravado. I know few adults who take compliments as well or who are as deserving.

You may think ten-year-old Doug was a pseudo-adult as ten-year-olds are apt to be in their hurry to grow up, but he was not. He was all boy, and all ten years old as he told the corny jokes only grade school kids can come up with and as he hopped, skipped and jumped his way over the landscape. No, this was not a kid who had grown up too soon. He was just a well-parented kid, a nice boy, a nice human being. Douglas, I'm glad I met ya.

§

But Are You Having Fun?

A friend of mine recently appeared with a sweatshirt that read...

He who dies with the most toys, wins!

It made me laugh and laugh, but I don't know why. It really isn't funny, so perhaps it was the truth it spoke that tickled my funny bone. We do all seem to be in a competition to accumulate more and more, especially grown up toys. The question is: do we really have more fun with those toys?

The saying "You can tell the men from the boys by the price of their toys" is truer than most of us would like to admit. Presumably, the more elaborate and the more expensive the toy, the more fun you can have with it. Really? Let's look at boating as an example, since I have had ample opportunity to play with such toys over the years.

By any real definition, sailing is the fine art of getting wet while slowly going nowhere at great expense. I leave the definition of motorboating up to your own imagination.

I have watched the captains of these vessels turn blue from cussing at the gas bills, the marina charges, the motor that breaks more than it works and the sails that never set without a hitch. Of course, the crews are never maximally obedient to the captain's orders, and are forever tracking up the freshly scrubbed decks.

"Now hear this. You will have fun and that is an order!" But have you noticed, people with expensive toys, be they boats, cars, electronics, or artwork, never let themselves or anyone else *really play* with these toys. Instead they always look brand-new, and are barely smudged by human fingerprints.

Kids don't seem much different from their adult counterparts, either. I was observing a two-year-old boy the other day as he ignored his toy box full of expensive and psychologically researched Fisher-Price toys. Instead of playing with them, he laid waste to the kitchen cupboards. For this child (and for me as a child, so my mother reports), the most fun was to empty out the lower cupboards of canned goods, pie tins, pots and pans. To these he took a wooden spoon and began a musical career in the drums.

I know families that have garage sales two and three times a year, just to unload all the toys the kids played with once on Christmas and once on their birthday and that was it. Of course, they pestered their parents to distraction for all those must-have objects everyone else was getting. Whether those toys were really fun to play with was irrelevant. The kids were already becoming indoctrinated in keeping up with the Joneses, so it should not be a surprise that the pattern persists intact into adulthood.

Let's take a look at Halloween. The tradition of dressing up in costumes is wonderful. It legitimizes the urge to act goofy and to dress like, if not act out, your fantasies. I'm always fascinated by the costumes people choose for Halloween, and since I don't think anything is an accident, I assume that the costume chosen says something about you or your secret self or your secret wishes for yourself. I include myself in this as well.

For example, I know a man who always dresses up as a racecar driver. He was one once, so he has all the gear, but more importantly, he wishes he still could race. A broken back and the responsibilities of his own business prevent him from pursuing this dream.

Then there is the chic, always fashionable beauty who dresses as a nerd. How wonderful it is not to have to coordinate colors and textures for a change. The skinny guy goes as a fat man; the shy conservative librarian as a hooker;

the hard-working and compulsive school teacher as a bum; the sweet, oppressed housewife as a witch.

Not all costumes are opposite to the day-to-day self. Many are just extensions or exaggerated versions of the person we see every day. The fastidious and fair-minded store manager goes as a surgeon, which he easily could be with his calm, measured responses for every crisis and his attention to detail. The playboy bunny is a nice girl with a mischievous streak she'd like to expose more often.

Even people who don't or won't dress up make a statement about what they won't or can't reveal and share about themselves. Now, lest I seem like a party-pooper by analyzing even the innocent fun of Halloween costuming, I want you to know I love to dress up and I love the creative concoctions others dream up. That I see more than is intended to be seen, or perhaps is even there, only adds to my pleasure. The infinite variety and complexity of people always delights me, keeps my curiosity tickled and is just plain fun.

There you have it. He who dies with the most toys wins only if he finds just plain fun in his life, with and without all his toys.

§

A Man's Castle

A man's home is his castle, so the saying goes, implying that it is where he has things the way he wants them, and that his wishes and desires reign supreme. That at least is the theory for what your home is supposed to do for you. It's rarely the reality.

One of the things your home does do for you is to tell the rest of the world things about you, things you might not otherwise choose to reveal. People look like their houses, or rather, a person's house looks like them.

When I bought a little solar adobe house recently, the general comment was "The house looks just like you, Carol!" I knew I liked it or I wouldn't have bought it, but did it really look like me? Yes, I guess it did.

It's solid, that is, short and stocky. It's natural. It's practical. It's warm. It is not pretty, fussy, delicate or high fashion. It is quite small, which doesn't fit my rather expansive and sometimes extravagant spirit. The smallness, however, is teaching me how to live with limitations, mine, others' and the house's, which is certainly a tolerance I have long needed to develop. So I guess it is me, or is the "me" I need to become.

Then there are people who live in huge rambling houses, some modern, some old-fashioned, and some a mixture of the two.

I recently met a person who restored a lovely old 1893 Victorian house in a nearby small town. Slowly but surely he is furnishing it with period pieces and has surrounded it with a rose garden complete with hand-laid circular brick walks, miniature fruit trees and a white wrought iron fence lined with purple lilac bushes.

It is the picture of small town tranquility with an air of elegance that whispers of servants to polish the banister and a gardener to nurture the rosebuds. This house tells much about its owner. Old-fashioned in his manners, he calls all females "ladies," holds the door for you, gives you his arm when walking and looks altogether prim and proper behind his Woody Allen glasses and short haircut.

You wouldn't guess such a nice quiet man could be a bearcat on the dance floor, but then Victorian houses were infamous for the secrets they hid behind all those potted palms and formal drawing room doors.

Historical houses reveal the owner's love, respect, even longing for the past; modern homes, perhaps a reaching for the future, presumably for something better than what has passed before.

The interiors of a home are also telltale of its owners. I have been in homes that are like museums. What wasn't under glass couldn't be touched and a dish was washed as soon as it was used. One spoke in whispers, sat on the edge of the chair and tip-toed around. One could only surmise that the owner was so frightened of his own impulses that not a hair could be allowed out of place for fear a floodgate of explosive emotion would break loose and wreak havoc.

Then there are those homes that resemble pig sties. They seem to me to be the inverse of the museum house. Here, lack of impulse control is evident everywhere. Occupants of these two kinds of houses are impulse ridden, one just over-controls it and the other lacks self control.

There is also the eclectic house and decor. The exterior and the interior are a hodge-podge of styles and tastes. Clean, but not pristine, it's a well-used and lived-in home. I know of just such a house and its owners.

Once world travelers, they have hung the bits and pieces of their sojourns all over their walls. Into antiques, drama and their church, they have collections, memorabilia and symbols of each covering every surface. It's a warm, inviting and fascinating home, as the owners are themselves.

Some argue that their house is only the shelter over their heads and that they put nothing of themselves into it. But I would argue that houses that show nothing, tell of owners who have nothing to show or have little to share.

Whether we like it or not, and whether we're aware of it or not, we tell the world who and what we are by the way we talk, the way we dress (and I don't mean fashion here), and by the place we call home.

If a man's home is his castle, then his castle *is* the man. So the next time you open your door to let someone into your house, remember you are letting them in on yourself as well.

§

But I Need It...I Need You...

"Carol, your house is soooooo small; don't you need more room?"

"Dear girl, your car is so old and crummy; don't you need a new one?"

"I just don't see how you can manage without a man around, at least some of the time. I need a man around to do all the things I can't do." (You male readers just substitute a woman here.)

"Of course, I need more money. Who doesn't! There is so much I want to do if only..." I answer.

So go the commiserations of my friends and acquaintances, but wait a minute. What was the last sentence? There is so much I want.... Ah huh! Caught ya! There's that word *want*, and isn't that the real truth. You want so much, but how much of it do you really *need*?

How many suits or dresses do you really need? Remember, you can only wear one suit at a time. Go to your closet. How many pieces get used frequently and how many just hang there week in and week out waiting for the just-in-case day?

Look into your kitchen cupboards. Do you really bake bread often? At all? Or do you have all those pans just in case someday the Mother Earth bug bites you?

For myself, I have pie dishes that have never and probably never will see the inside of my oven. I have soufflé dishes, quiche dishes and cake pans that I have never used. I guess it's time to admit I'll never be a baker or a gourmet cook.

When I was a park ranger in the Colorado wilderness, I used one old, huge stew/soup pot and one good frying pan, and I never looked once under the sink for all the other pans I lugged all those miles. It was a revelation to me. My poor car had been so loaded down with three of everything for any contingency, and I never used even one third of it.

Backpacking is a good way to learn how little you really need vs. how much you want. After carrying all those extra items you packed just-in-case for five or ten miles, you learn to toss half aside the next time you venture forth.

One of the reasons I keep my big ole frumpy station wagon is because I can travel with everything but the kitchen sink. When I unpack three-quarters of it unused, as I always do, I marvel at the persistence of my wants and my repeated refusal to see what it is I really need and don't need.

My little house is teaching me a lot in this area. Yes, it would be nice to have more room, but if I did, I'd just fill it up with more junk, more antiques to dust and oil, more books to join all the others I still haven't read and more projects I'll start and never finish.

As for *needing* another person in my life vs. *wanting* him.... Yes, I want a lovely, erudite, talented man to brighten my days, just as most of the men I know want a lovely, erudite, talented woman in theirs. But needing that companionship is something else.

Think of the widows, widowers and divorcees who thought they couldn't make it alone. In the wake of their loss, they emerge like butterflies from a cocoon. As they discover themselves anew or for the first time, they find each day is an adventure. As they explore all the things they can

157

do and could have done if only they hadn't shackled themselves with false assumptions of need, they become delighted with themselves. The men learn to cook and even become gourmets. Women tackle finances, legalese and forsake their nails to oil and lube their cars.

Sorting out what it is you really need vs. what you really want can be an exciting process.

I used to have so many wants I thought were needs that chasing them occupied at least half my waking hours and most of my dreaming hours. It was a terrible burden, and the worst part was that I never seemed satisfied. No matter how many of those *needs* I fulfilled, I always seemed to need more. I was just like the mindless donkey chasing the dangling carrot.

Then one day I stopped and realized that I didn't need the carrot, that I had everything I needed already. Now the job was to sort out what it was I really wanted. To do that, I imagined that I knew I was going to die in one month's time. What then, I asked myself, was the most important thing I wanted to get into my life in the time remaining?

The answer did not contain one single thing. The answer had to do with people, friends and love.

Think of the obituaries you read. Not a one details all the clothes or cars or houses a person accumulated in his or her lifetime, thinking he needed them. The accolades are about all the time that person spent with and for others. Think about your own obituary. What five or six words on your gravestone would say it all? How do you want to be remembered? Now that, I contend, is where your real *needs* lie and all the rest are *wants*.

§

Do All Things Come to Him Who Waits?

"All comes to him who waits." This is an admonition I've heard more times than I can count, since patience is not one of my virtues.

All my life I've been a gung-ho humdinger of a go-getter. (Is that English?) I became that way because I had parents like that. Our family believed in the legendary Protestant work ethic, which made you nervous if even your play time wasn't scheduled with creative and worthwhile projects. I own a book titled, "How to make the most of your leisure time"! However, I have not read it.

When I do finally crash and spend a whole day on the couch reading a book, I usually have to be sick or, at the very least, say I threw the day away or wasted the day doing nothing. I'm not alone.

I know all kinds of folks like me, trapped in the guilt of nonproductivity. If you're not productive, you're taking up valuable space someone else could use. How then do I reconcile this wonderful advice that seems to be completely true: "All comes to him who waits"?

Waiting, for me, is agony. I want to learn to go with the flow, but how do you do it? How do you know when to wait and when to move? Timing seems to be critical to everything and yet there are no rules, just your instincts. When you have a personality like mine, your instincts can do you in.

When a male friend turned to me for comfort after he'd blown yet another potential love affair because he moved too fast, I was all sympathy. It's hard to go slow when you're sure you are in love. After all, the Love Boat romances work out in the length of a cruise, don't they?

Then there was the three-month period it took to close the sale of the little house I just bought. The seller moved out of town, I moved in and then we discovered no legal easement to the property existed.

It fell to me, a first-time know-nothing buyer, to get all the previous owners and neighbors involved, to sign all the rewritten contracts, deeds and easements. Keeping everyone moving forward on the mess while at the same time taking care not to reveal my frustration by pushing too hard was a balancing act I hope never to repeat.

If I hadn't kept at it, we'd still be hanging fire, but if I had pushed any harder, I probably would have alienated everyone and ruined the whole deal. Salesmen must wrestle with this dilemma all the time. You can't sell if you don't push, and yet if you push too much too soon, you won't make a sale either.

What about you dieters? Because you are impatient, diet scheme after diet scheme bilks you for hundreds of dollars. The creators of these schemes cater to that impatience. You can almost hear the circuslike barker hawking his sideshow. "Come on, ladies and gents, sign right up. Lose ten pounds in ten days, guaranteed. Be the person you dream of, overnight." And sure enough, you take the bait, lose weight and put twice the amount back on in the next six months.

Ah, Homo sapiens, thy name is impatience, but then where would the species be if we weren't fast movers and go-getters? Where does patience end and lost opportunity begin? How do you know when to walk and when to run? How do you learn when to hold your tongue and when to speak up? When is silence golden and when does it turn to an entrapping quagmire?

I know the best way to get through life is one step at a time, but at what pace? When do you get ahead by actually standing still? If it is true that all comes to him who waits, the "him" will have to have a lot of time. I'm not that young anymore; time is running out. Yet if I'm always moving my life along at a good pace, what will I miss because I didn't learn to wait and let life come to me?

The answer, I suspect, is to learn to go with the flow, but how? I'm working on it.

§

WINTER

§

Going with the Flow

What is this "going with the flow" that sounds so wonderful but is so elusive to define, let alone nail down and follow? I'm reminded of the advice fathers bequeath to their sons. "Learn to roll with the punches, my boy. You'll get fewer black eyes that way."

But that isn't quite the same as going with the flow. To flow, after all, is by all authoritative accounts "to drift, to glide, to slide, to go along with, to ripple, to gurgle, to move around or pass and not resist." That last is the one I resonate to the best...to not resist.

Going with the flow isn't a matter of bouncing back from a blow, but rather sensing deep down in those recesses of your mind, heart or soul the gentle shifts of the times and events in your life. If you are thusly in tune with yourself, you have help on when to move and when to wait, when to fight and when to give up, on any particular issue. You sense the direction and then go with it, not resisting.

When I'm trying to understand a difficult concept, I often turn to analogies because concrete images help me get a grasp on the abstract, and going with the flow is really an abstract idea. It is not something you can see but only feel, and even that is difficult.

I think of people who, in the past, lived so closely to the land that they lived more by instinct and spontaneous wit than by calculation. They flowed with the signals from all their senses.

Long before a storm was at all evident they could smell it coming and act accordingly. Impending danger made the hair on the backs of their necks bristle even when all appeared tranquil. To survive they had to be completely in touch with themselves and the subtleties of their gut reactions.

However, if you are going to listen to your instincts, then you had better trust them. That is tricky. So often I've had a feeling about something and then immediately ignored it, only to catch myself saying later, "You know, I had a feeling that would happen, or I should have...."

Ah yes, the infamous "I knew I should have...." This feeling is probably some of the best evidence of you *not* going with the flow you'll ever find. And that is probably one way to discover what going with the flow is—by studying when or what it is not. Each time you catch yourself saying, "I knew I should have," or, "I just had a feeling," that is probably the moment of the flow you chose to ignore or resist.

There is also more to this than just going with one's instincts. After all, you could argue that I am advocating being impulsive, which I am not. Reasoned spontaneity would be more like it.

There is a process to life, I believe, and while I can't tell you exactly what it is, I do have a faith that helps me through the blind spots and those days when I don't understand why things are as they are.

For those who subscribe to a particular religious belief, I guess I am talking about their faith...in the will of God, of Allah, of Buddha, of Mother Earth and Father Sky. For those who do not subscribe to a formal religion or belief system, there is still a process that is life, and accepting life as it comes to you, however you explain it, is the *flow* I am trying so hard to understand.

Going with the flow is opening up to life, not closing off for fear of hurtful surprises.

Going with the flow is taking risks and being truly willing to accept the consequences.

Going with the flow is being knocked off your feet and instead of getting up right away—mad as hell and ready to fight—sitting still for a moment, taking time to look around and see what your world looks like from that perspective.

Going with the flow is seeing a break in your path not as a brief detour but as an opportunity to go in a whole new direction you might never have considered otherwise.

Going with the flow is learning how to let go and grab onto life at the same time.

§

Nothing Ventured, Nothing Gained

You may have noticed by now that I'm in love with language and especially so with the colloquialisms, slogans and everyday tidbits of wisdom and advice we fling at each other without thinking, unfortunately.

I think about them because I listen to people with a third ear, so let's look at one of my favorites: "nothing ventured, nothing gained." Every time a boy or man approaches a new female he'd like to know, he must gather up his courage and take the chance: the chance of what? That he might be rejected or that he might be accepted and then need to risk even more.

Every time a salesman calls on a new prospective customer, he risks being ignored, brushed off, and turned down. Or he risks making a sale and then, by golly, his product had better be as good as he said it was.

Every time a woman flirts with a man, she risks having her advances given a cold shoulder or that they work, the man takes the bait, and now she must be as attractive within as she is without.

The businessperson dreams of having his own operation, so he risks everything, gets the money, and now must deliver and be as good as his dream, or fail.

It seems to me that in all these examples and in any others you can think of, taking chances is a double-edged sword. It can cut you both ways. If you fail, the dejection and blow to your self-esteem can range from mild to devastating. The fear of rejection and failure seems to be a universal anxiety in all men.

But I would also contend that the fear of success is at least equally potent, even if generally denied. And denied it is. Just go to any bookstore and look at the hundreds of books on how to succeed or win at this, that, or the other thing. Then try to find the one lonely volume on fear of success. Everyone loves a winner, so how can anyone be afraid to succeed? The idea is absurd. But is it?

To succeed, after all, be it in interpersonal encounters, business or social arenas, means you now must be what you've always dreamed of, what you always said you could be, if only. Dreams, after all, are free, and words are cheap. But behavior can tell all, and now with success, you must live up to your dreams. No more puffed up protests of "if only, then I could...." The "if only" day has come, so how are you going to handle it?

It is my observation that people do not handle success well. Because we are accustomed to or expecting failure, success comes as a shock and the reaction seems to be equally extreme.

The successful person can go to the extreme of becoming arrogant or can go the other way, undoing his success with self-deprecating comments and gestures. Compliments are waved away, accolades countered by deflecting credit to undeserving others, and obsessive worries about not deserving all this good luck dominate waking and sleeping hours.

Before you know it, the success starts to dwindle away, completing the self-fulfilling prophecy of "this was all too good to be true, and I didn't deserve it." Well, maybe you didn't, or at least didn't think you did.

If it is true that you are what you think, then maybe you make your own luck with your own attitude. Be careful here. You have to be very honest with yourself about those attitudes. You can spend days dreaming about success, but if deep down in your heart you really don't believe it can happen, or that you don't deserve it, then you won't get it. I don't think your thoughts are magic, but I do think your attitudes are more powerful than either you or I have ever imagined.

The trouble is we are usually only in touch with those attitudes and feelings that live on the surface, in the conscious mind, readily available. And it has been my experience that it is the underlying, the deeply buried attitudes and feelings, long suppressed in the unconscious, that are the more powerful and the real determining factors in the consequences of our lives.

Because those unconscious feelings are so hard to get in touch with, we often feel that our lives are out of control and that we are buffeted hither and yon by the external forces of life.

But, in fact, we may be more in control of our lives than we know. The difficult part of this is admitting that maybe the misfortune in our lives is caused by ourselves as much as the fortune is. That hurts. It's always easier and certainly more comfortable to blame others, the ill winds of fate, and just bad luck.

But maybe, just maybe, we orchestrate our own undoing. If that is true, then we can also turn our misfortunes around, we can build from the ruins, we can author our own successes and deserve them all. But first you must venture into your soul and take a long, hard look. I promise you if you do, you have everything to gain and nothing to lose.

§

Hidden Blessings

Why are the holidays so hard on everyone? By definition, holiday means time out from the daily grind and worries. The holidays are supposed to be a time of harmony and love; a time of giving and receiving; a time when goodwill overrides the animosities that have accumulated over the months, perhaps even over the years.

Feuding partners are supposed to lay down their swords. Rivaling siblings are supposed to become pals. Bosses are supposed to show their employees how much they appreciate them and vice versa. Generations are supposed to gather, and in so doing, renew the continuity of the ages.

It is the "supposed to" aspect of all this that is the rub. Rarely is life as it is supposed to be according to the mythology of tradition, the media hype, and the wishes most of us harbor in our hearts.

It would be nice if peace and love reigned within and between individuals, families and nations, but the fact is, they don't. The history of man is not one of harmony and goodwill, but of competition and aggression, mostly on the pettiest of levels.

I think it is this disparity between the dream and the reality that makes the holidays so hard. Those who are struggling economically sink to their knees trying to purchase those glittering and supposed evidences of love confronting them at every turn of the television dial. The holiday merchandising barrage seems to mock the poor and even the struggling middle class.

Those who have enough money to buy most of the gifts they want to give are faced with the imaginary equation between price tag and love. Does last year's gift have to be bettered to prove continuing love? Will diamond earrings or a Rolex watch make up for a year of neglect and lack of involvement in the marriage or family? Does the price tag prove affection (I care enough to spend a lot of my hard-earned money on you), or does it become a buy-off for not being willing to give of yourself and your time?

Unfortunately, I think the buy-off happens more often than not. After all, a one-time extravagant shot is a lot easier than is the day-in and day-out giving of yourself. How do you show that off to anyone? It isn't very visible except to you, and even then you can become blinded by taking it for granted. It isn't flashy nor can it be hauled out on special occasions to impress others. There is no price tag to accidentally leave on, nor can it be placed under a tree as one of the many things Santa left you.

Yet I would wager that for every fancy, high-priced item unwrapped, the receiver would gladly turn it back if, in exchange, he or she received daily love, support and friendship.

Loneliness is the number one killer of souls (and sometimes bodies), especially during the holidays. All the party glitter, presents and media fantasies cannot obscure the reality that life is mostly a plain affair and that the gifts that count the most must be given on a daily basis, week in and month out.

The homemade jams, pickles, breads and crafts are far superior gifts than are the latest manufacturers' creations. A person's time and sweat has gone into those gifts. You, the receiver of such gifts, were thought about long before the holiday advertising began.

In that way, the poor man has it over the rich. Because he can't buy a lot, the poor man is, out of necessity, forced to give more of himself. Having to give of oneself is a blessing in disguise, for it blesses both the giver and receiver. It is one gift we all can afford to give.

§

Promises, Promises

One of the myths of the Wild West was that a man was as good as his word and contracts were sealed with only a handshake. Unfortunately, a man's word, the almighty promise, has fallen on hard times. There is nothing like the Christmas and New Year holidays to illustrate this.

To a child, the promise is sacred. Any parent knows that if he has promised his small child something, he had better make good on that promise or lose status in his adoring child's esteem.

To adults, breaking a promise may be human, but to a child, it is tantamount to being a villain, a dastardly evil-doer, a crusher of pure hope, faith and trust. It behooves all of us to take care with those three little words, "I promise you," and especially so when promising a child.

Even adults take offense when promises are broken. A man is supposed to be as good as his word, and while adults are supposed to be more understanding and forgiving, I think the child's reaction of shock and disbelief still lurks in the recesses of even the most mature of adults.

"But you promised you'd stop working such long hours. You promised we'd have a vacation this year. You promised to keep control of your spending. You promised you'd call. You promised to love me forevermore. You promised. You promised!"

In anger and tears, the accusations of broken promises are laid out like so many corpses over time, taking on the proportions of a massacre. Why are so many promises broken?

And of all the promises made, promises to ourselves seem to have the least potency, yet should be the most important. Perhaps it is because the shame of a broken promise is private this time. You have only yourself to face.

If all your New Year's resolutions go down the drain, well, you can make a joke of it, shrug your shoulders and promise that next year you'll do better. But there you go again, making promises.

When I was a kid, the way you caught someone in a lie or half-truth was to say, "Do you promise that's so? Do you promise? Come on, *promise!*" We kids knew that to promise falsely was to bring down the wrath of all the gods that ever lived. It was more serious than swearing, and that was very heavy stuff, too, in the 1950s.

I can't remember when I first realized that promises were not sacred. Probably about the same time I realized that Santa Claus was not a real person. That day is crystal clear. I was home sick and tucked into the living room couch, the best place to secure maximum maternal attention.

I must have been overhearing snatches of conversations over those weeks preceding my seventh Christmas, when suddenly the collective message came to me. In disbelief I asked my mother, "Is Santa Claus real?"

Her hedged, diplomatic answer fell on deaf ears. I was crushed. It was one of the biggest promises ever made to me and now it was broken. A huge chunk of my childhood was hacked away that fateful afternoon, and the bitter-sweet reality of growing up became the healing scar tissue.

When promises are made to me today, and then broken, that old scar tissue aches as it tries to stretch and be flexible. I try not to make too many promises myself. The child in me still takes them much too seriously. Instead, I promise I'll *try* to be as good as my word and that, after all, is all any of us can really do.

Each New Year's Day, I promise myself to be a little better person than I was the past year, and that is a promise I know I can keep. After all, I've gotten generous in my old age. I give myself the entire year to do it and I have only myself to disappoint...and forgive.

That's one of the really nice things about growing up. You learn to forgive, to accept yourself and others for all those human imperfections. What a relief it is to surrender childhood perfectionism!

§

The Letdown

So, tell me, what was it all for? The months of shopping; weeks of planning and decorating; days and days of baking; what were they all for?

The anticipation of Christmas is so high. The dreams of love and appreciation that must surely come for all your thoughtful gifts are so warming. The anticipated comrade-ship of friends, colleagues and family feels so close it nearly chokes you. Then that fateful day arrives, the day when all that is good between people is supposed to reach its climax.

For some, Christmas Day is wonderful and all one's expectations are fulfilled. For others, the disappointment is like the proverbial pebble in your shoe. By the end of the day it has become a rock that has bruised you and slowed your pace to a crawl.

In either event, and for all the levels in between, the day after is a horrendous letdown experienced by everyone, it seems. If you don't have to go to work, you will probably spend the majority of the day lying around and sleeping. If you do go to the office, you and everyone else will go through your tasks like zombies, accomplishing little.

The letdown after Christmas seems to be a common experience and doesn't seem to be related to whether you had a good or bad day. Rather, it appears to me to be the flip side of the same coin as anticipation.

For example, planning and packing for a trip and even the journey itself always takes longer than the return trip does. Climbing a mountain takes longer and is so much more challenging than coming down.

Courting, the wedding and the honeymoon all must end—and they usually do—with a sobering thud. Flowers fade, leaves fall off the trees, and the earth sleeps under the mantle of winter. It is the natural rhythm of life that things must come to a spontaneous ending.

Christmas is the celebration of a new life, of the beginning of Christianity, and yet it comes at the end of Christendom's calendar year. Hidden then, in all the festivities, is the sting of farewells, the heaviness of grieving.

Just as winter brings an end to the previous seasons of birth, growth and harvest, so does Christmas signal the end of a year of dreams, plans and promises that may or may not have been fulfilled.

Marriages were made and ended. Children were born and children died. Lovers came and went. Business deals were made while others crumbled. Members of the older generation passed their torches to their seed.

It is fitting, I think, that New Year's follows so closely on the heels of all this accounting. Endings are beginnings, too. Letting go is the key to new life. It is hard to see the light at the end of the tunnel.

We seem to spend so much of our time in darkness, groping our way toward vague and ill-defined goals or dreams. But the light is there even if you can't see it on that day after when you feel so let down. The crash is normal, it is necessary, it should be anticipated. You just have to remember as you are overwhelmed by exhaustion and melancholy, that this day may be the end of a year in your life, but it is also the first day of the rest of your life, and that means anything is possible.

§

Life Isn't Fair

Life isn't fair. Wherever did I get the idea it was? Somebody sold me, and you, I suspect, a bill of goods about all those rewards we'd glean if we kept ourselves on the straight and narrow, always doing the right thing. Well, it just isn't so. The good are not rewarded and the bad are not punished.

The Peter Principle is really true. People are promoted beyond their level of competence and effectiveness, creating a bottleneck that stops, frustrates and defeats the truly qualified from going where they should or at least could, if only....

Annual political elections always make me laugh about this. The campaign slogans never seem to change. "It's time for honest, informed leadership. It's time to elect leaders who think for themselves and who are not swayed by special interests." Blah, blah, blah.

I thought that was what we voted for the last time. Who lied? Or are we willingly duped into believing that if you make it to the top, you must be good?

Well, it just isn't so. I have worked in large institutions and small, in the public domain and the private sector, and I'm here to tell you no place is safe. Idiots and tyrants abound, and they do so in the highest echelons of government, private corporations, academia and small enterprises alike.

I am thinking of a professor who cannot file, and therefore can never find, his personal papers like insurance, mortgages and taxes. He cannot pay a bill on time, nor can he finish anything he starts, at work or at home.

I am thinking of government bureaucrats with whom I once worked. Well, actually I worked, and their work consisted of sending my work back time and again to change a comma or a word here and there so they could maintain the facade of supervision and still drink coffee all day.

I'm thinking of a flower shop owner I used to know years ago. She went through employees like the flowers she tossed out as soon as the bloom came off the rose. She complained endlessly about their incompetence, yet it was she who was the incompetent employer.

The professor will become a much-honored emeritus, the bureau chief will enter politics and probably become a governor or senator, and the flower shop owner will create her own franchise.

So what then do you do to keep yourself from filling up with resentment at the injustices of life? I think the answer is in where and how you expect justice and fairness.

We'd like to think we've progressed from the eye-for-an-eye and tooth-for-a-tooth days of Babylon, but we haven't, not really. Deep, down inside we love violence and its swiftness. If you doubt me, just look at the proliferation of violence on television and in the cinema. The bad guys get theirs, most without the laborious grinding of the gears of the judicial system. If that is not enough, consider capital punishment—a life for a life. It's as simple as that.

However, except for capital executions, the wish for such swift and violent justice is mostly fantasy. For the most part, the judicial systems of the world work and are needed for the major offenses against society. The little injustices of life that most of us endure in silence are only rectified in our revenge fantasies.

Even in these seemingly harmless imaginings, I think we are barking up the wrong tree. When you become concerned, preoccupied, even consumed with thoughts of revenge, you poison only your own world. Since most people do not act out their fantasies of revenge, the time and energy they spend on such thoughts costs only them. It costs the object of your ire nothing.

While you are spending time dreaming up neat ways to get even, you cannot spend that time dreaming of the ways you will create all the good things you want for yourself. If you spend time hating, then hate becomes a powerful force and presence in your life.

In other words, you are what you think, and if you think about hatred, revenge and unfairness much of the time, then of course you will see that everywhere you go.

"Where, then, is justice," you want to scream in your frustration. It must exist somewhere, or the concept would not be an integral part of the history of mankind. Recorded history usually ascribes the role of final judge to the highest authorities, either within a society or to a religiously defined God.

Traditionally, justice comes from an outside source, a higher power, an ultimate judge. But I don't think so. I think justice and all its adjoining punishments and rewards come from within each individual. I think you make your own heaven and hell, even when it is not evident to others and sometimes not even to yourself. If I am right, then "he'll" get his in the end, and so will you. Put your energies into yourself, not into worrying about the other guy's comeuppance.

§

Keeping Perspective

A few years ago I shared Christmas with a family from France, and relearned an important lesson I learned twenty years before when I went to the University of Vienna in Austria. That lesson was that the American way is not the only way of doing things, nor is it necessarily the best way, though we tend to think it is.

I wanted to give stockings stuffed to their limits, in addition to a couple of Southwestern presents to our visitors. But the French I was told, did not make such a big deal of Christmas, and so many gifts would have embarrassed them and perhaps carried meanings to them that I did not intend.

As I unpacked those stockings and scaled down my holiday giving, I was forced to reflect on the American way of overgiving. Are we really hapless victims of commercialization unable to control our spending, or has our affluence deluded us into thinking we can buy affection and acceptance instead of working for it on a daily basis?

I suspected the latter and, as painful as it was to admit, I suspected myself of just that with these visitors whom I wanted to impress. Ouch! I thought I had conquered that one.

Crossing the language barrier was another one of those tough lessons I learned long ago and managed to forget in my snug and smug existence. It is not one I should have forgotten, for living in the Southwest I am confronted daily with at least the Spanish language and often several American Indian languages.

Yet here I was, struggling to communicate with my nonexistent French and my friends' elementary English and an abundance of hand signs. To make matters worse, I shouted my slow, laborious sentences as if their lack of comprehension meant that they were also deaf. I, too, had been shouted at in Austria when I couldn't understand German, so I should have known better. How embarrassing.

All that struggling to communicate reminded me why the world is no further along than it is. It is hard work to communicate to and be understood by another culture, even one as closely akin to ours as the French. It's much easier to stay at home and talk to your neighbor than it is to make a place for a foreigner at your dinner table.

I often spend Thanksgiving with a family who invites one or two foreign students from the nearby university to share this American holiday with them. It's hard work controlling the dinner table banter among close friends so that the guests from Africa, Asia, or South America can be kept in the flow of conversation. Most of us are too lazy to try such sharing more than once, if that.

I took a walk with one of the French visitors after Christmas dinner in an effort to undo the damage I had just done at the table and to have a chance at quiet conversation.

I spoke slowly. He listened carefully. I redefined all the big words and slang expressions I used without realizing it. He repeated what I said to see if he understood my meanings.

It was hard work for both of us. At one point we were interrupted by a jet flying high overhead. He pointed to the speck in the sky and said, "Two hundred people, two hundred people. We [are] so small, unimportant." Having traveled to America for the first time and traversed our great land by bus, this Frenchman was impressed by the great distances of our country.

He had taken note of his own existence and the speck he represents in all of mankind, past and present. He wanted to share that with me. He wanted to speak of such things, as difficult as it was to try. He reaffirmed my belief that all men struggle with the same basic issues, regardless of their economic, religious or cultural membership.

Our shared Christmas gave us more than congenial companionship. It gave us the mutual gift of a fresh perspective on our lives.

§

The Truth in Play

Have you ever stood back and watched a child play? If uninhibited by your presence, that child will tell you more truth about herself and her world in a few short minutes than she could ever tell you in a direct conversation. How adults play can be equally revealing for those with an eye to see it.

In the first place, the mode of play is very important. The person who chooses tennis over bridge already reveals a preference for a physical expression of himself rather than an intellectual expression. The stamp collector may be a gentle soul concerned with details and with this smallest chronicle of history. It is with tender loving care that he handles his treasures with tweezers as he studies them under a magnifying glass.

This man's play is a far cry from that of the weekend football or baseball warrior who loves the smell of sweat as he uses all his large muscles to execute his skill. The roar of the crowd, the chatter of his teammates, the primal gratification of chewing a huge wad of gum or tobacco with an open mouth, all gives vent to his pent-up frustrations and feels all-over good.

Play can be solitary, as in reading, painting art, listening to or making music or swimming laps in a pool. And it can graduate to small or large groups, i.e., the bridge game to the bridge tournament, the golf match to the golf tournament, the string quartet to the symphony. But the way you choose to spend your leisure time is not all there is to this. *How* you play at what you play is equally, if not more, revealing.

All football players are not alike. The tackler is a different breed of cat from the quarterback. Some choir members sing with little facial or body expression, while others act out the musical message, at least on their faces. Parlor games such as monopoly and scrabble attract both the screamers and the deadpan strategists.

There are tennis players who take the bad shots and missed points in stride and there are players who play for blood. Their competitiveness goes beyond healthy sportsmanship to serious aggression and temper tantrums inappropriate to the concept of play.

I recently watched a brief demonstration of pool. After watching me and a couple of others miss shot after shot, our host left his stamp collection, strode to the table, took a stick and with no more study of the table than that, hit a ball that ricocheted off four sides and found its home. A second equally spectacular shot sank two more balls.

I was fascinated. I had not suspected this quiet, soft-spoken, stamp-collecting, gourmet cook of sinful desserts to be the possessor of such precise aggression. There was no timidity in those shots, no hesitation, no doubt. Nor was there any discernible study of the task at hand. The table had been sized up in a second and the play executed with cool, almost grim, calculation.

I was impressed, not only by the admirable skill, but because of what it told me about the person. Let's just say that I'd want to be on his side in a fight.

Psychologists say that play is children's work. As they play, children learn and practice those skills they will need when they grow up. Well, you know what they say—practice makes perfect. So here's looking at you, even when you're not looking.

§

The Gardeners of Life

I've always been fond of using gardens as metaphors. For example, there are people who, like gardeners, specialize in various stages of planting, tending and harvesting.

Some people are the *plowers*, the first to break the ground, the pioneers. They scout out new territory and blaze the first trails for others to follow. These are the people who first suggest the unthinkable, who ring the first bells of warning while the rest of us sleep. These are the people who first shout into the wind of ignorance, complacency and tradition.

Then there are the people who are the *sowers* of seeds. While not the first on the scene, they are some of the early investors, eager to plant the first seedlings and to tend the young crop until it can stand on its own. These are the folks who head up new social, political or cultural programs once the legislation has been passed and funding is secured.

Not exactly pioneers, they are the early settlers. However, once the crop in the garden is fully established and on its way to harvest, these people often move on. The work that excites them the most is finished. These are the people who settle a new town and move on when the population grows bigger than the number of people you can know on a first-name basis.

Enter the *harvester*. These are the people who come at the end of the growing season. They are the finishers, the people who can settle in for the long haul. While the pioneers cut the road and the early settlers build the first schools and churches, the harvesters expand those schools and churches, build the universities and bring the polishing touches that define the concept of civilization.

It seems to me that if you can see yourself in one of these broad categories of gardeners even in today's complicated world, then you can look anew at some of your complaints about your life.

For example, if you are a harvester and like the security of civilization, then you shouldn't be surprised if your life is boring more often than not. Security, by definition, is not exciting.

The sowers of seeds may often have a feeling of incompleteness. Loving the excitement of seeing a new project get off the ground, they move on before the harvest, never seeing the fruits of their labors to maturity. Still, this is the price one pays for being a sower.

What of the pioneer, the entrepreneur who always seeks new ground to break? These are the most restless of all. They are the movers and shakers. These are the people who make us uncomfortable because of their prodding and pushing. They just can't leave well enough alone. And because they are the first to sound the alarm or ask the forbidden questions, they are rarely appreciated or thanked until long after they are dead, if then. It can be a very exciting but very lonely way to live.

Which kind of gardener are you, and what parallels can you draw to your work and to your relationships? Surprised?

§

Growing Up Is Hard to Do

There have been several interviews on television in the past six weeks that have absolutely astounded me. Barbara Walters interviewed three women—Sally Fields, Farrah Fawcett, and Shelley Long—and David Hartman interviewed Kathryn Hepburn. All four interviews revealed one common denominator: that growing up is hard to do for everyone, even the rich and famous.

Sally Fields talked about how she, at forty-plus years and after a failed marriage and many false starts in romance, finally has an inkling of what real, mature partnering may be. In fact she feels good enough about it and about herself to try marriage again. She also revealed that the relationship between fathers and daughters, children and their parents, is still an enigma to her, but at least she has given up performing for parental love. How many of us can say that?

Farrah Fawcett and Shelley Long both are expecting babies and spoke thoughtfully about finally feeling ready to take on this awesome responsibility. With so many teenagers having babies willy nilly, it's nice to see some adults really thinking about the importance of parenthood.

The point, however, is that after many career and personal triumphs and failures, they both felt grown-up enough to take on this ultimate adult role. Fawcett in particular talked about having at long last given up her dependency on her parents, with whom until recently she consulted daily when making decisions about her life and career. It is so hard to let go.

The most revealing interview was between David Hartman and Kathryn Hepburn. Hepburn said that from the first success she ever achieved in films, she turned all her paychecks over to her father who then managed her money for her and gave her an allowance! This continued until his death in the 1960s, at which point her father's secretary took over. Only recently had Hepburn assumed full responsibility for her own money. She was in her 70s.

When I heard that, I nearly fell down. Here is a woman who has been the personification of a female independent spirit for several generations. Were all those roles and her much-touted choice to be single all illusion?

Hepburn said the reason for the allowance arrangement was that she was simply irresponsible with money and apparently had elected not to change. Why should she? Her daddy would do it for her and, by her own admission, she liked pleasing him by doing it his way. It is sort of like Sally's song and dance for her father.

You may not find it strange that an adult would be tied to her father's apron strings all her life, but I do, especially when that adult has presented herself as a pioneer in women's self-assertion. Maybe Kate Hepburn was not really so independent after all. Maybe she loved a married man whose faith did not allow him to divorce and marry her because she never really wanted to grow up and let go of her daddy's hand. Yes, I know she had married earlier, but it didn't last.

It so happens that all these interviews were with women probably because it would be the rare man indeed who could reveal publicly his own doubts and struggles to grow up. Males in our society, after all, are supposed to be big boys and not cry or need their mothers once they are out of diapers. And perhaps it is this inappropriate and excessive pressure on men to grow up early and without a hitch that has resulted in the recently coined *Peter Pan Syndrome*. It is a pop-psychology diagnosis for men who don't grow up.

It seems then that growing up is very hard to do for everyone. And I thought I was alone. Now, if only we understood what being grown-up really means.

§

The Good in Bad

From time immemorial, man has struggled to understand and give purpose to the tragedies that beset him and his fellow inhabitants of earth. Whether natural or man-made, disasters on the individual as well as on the mass scale give man pause and cause him to question why. Why do bad things happen to good people; why do the good die young; why do the innocent suffer while the wicked eat cake?

The mass suffering in North Africa has rocked the world back on its heels once again. From crippled and terminally ill children, to teenagers and church groups, to the six thousand individuals who have answered the Peace Corps call, the citizens of the world have responded to the suffering of their fellow man.

Therein may be the first inkling of the blessing in this huge curse. It has always been the story of man that he is at his best (and sometimes his worst) when stretched and challenged by adversity. When natural disaster strikes, the citizens of many nations reach beyond their nationality to join the family of man and grasp the hand of their human brothers and sisters.

Every problem comes bearing a gift, they say, even huge problems, so what can be the gift of such massive suffering like that in Africa decade after decade? Perhaps the answer can be found in the testimony of Edward Kennedy after his visit to Ethiopian refugee camps. In the face of total despair and loss, he found grace, courage and hope. Against all odds, the refugees traversed the most hostile of environments—drought compounded by civil war —fueled only by their hope and their wish to survive.

Against all odds, an army of volunteers waged war against the ultimate enemies, starvation and disease, to try to grant that wish to live. And through it all, the soldiers of politics and self-aggrandizement ignored life in favor of winning a make-believe war.

So, is that the gift of this tragedy? Warriors of hate taking lives, and opposing warriors of love trying to save the same lives?

There is ironic poetry in the Kennedy trip. Individuals whose lives have known tragedy that touched the world now reach out to a tragic world to return some of the support they once received. Having once been intimately connected to the family of man through their own suffering and loss of life, they now seek to restore that connection, however they are able.

I can't help but wonder if that longing to be intensely connected to the human race, to the larger family of man, isn't what suffering makes available to us as nothing else seems to. The pain of others reaches out like the ripples in a pond to touch the lives of so many. It touches those who know little of pain and it touches those who have their own private hells. But to each, the suffering of so many asks that they reach beyond their complacency or their own preoccupations to see themselves in a larger context.

Not since the charismatic John F. Kennedy made the call-to-service challenge in his inaugural address have so many risen out of the entrapment of their own narrow existence to give themselves to strangers halfway around the world.

The intoxicant of doing something useful for others has infected their blood. And predictably, the extent of the response seems to be proportionate to the tragedy at hand. Big good seems to come from big bad. Is this what it takes to teach the world that we are all of the same family, all on the same island-earth, all of the same fate?

Ten years ago the drought in Malaysia got lots of money response, but not lots of people response. I guess we didn't get the message the first time (or was that the tenth time?).

Could the message be that we must love life, all life, more than we hate starvation and death? That the only gift that really makes a difference is the gift of oneself?

§

The Weighty Truth

It has happened...again. We have a new disease—obesity. And when you label something a disease, you can comfortably absolve yourself from responsibility for your own body and your own health.

This business of legitimatizing bad habits and emotional neediness by calling them diseases so the individual can stop feeling guilty never ceases to discourage me.

I feel the same way about alcoholism as I do this obesity-as-a-disease bit. You don't catch alcoholism or obesity. It is something you do to yourself and the only effective treatment is to stop doing it to yourself. Pills, shots, hospitalization all work temporarily, but in the long run there is only one thing that makes the real difference—the individual and his inner commitment to change.

Alcoholics Anonymous is the only effective and long-standing treatment for alcoholism because people talking to and caring for people fills the need and punctures the loneliness vacuum that the booze once filled. Yes, yes, I do know about genetic predispositions, but a predisposition is only a factor to contend with and is not a destiny cast in stone.

Look at the proliferation of weight-control and diet plans in this country. We are people obsessed with our weight, and yet the very fact that new diets are coming out every day attests to our consummate failure in finding any lasting answers.

It was inevitable that the medical profession would get into the act at some point. By golly, if you've got a disease, who can blame you for your abusive eating habits? My disease makes me do it.

I do not quarrel with the evidence that being overweight contributes to stress and the deterioration of one's overall health. When you add a lot of weight to your frame, there is no question that all your parts have to work harder and will wear out sooner. But clearly, going at this problem from a purely physical point of view has not worked to date. So let's try another tack. It certainly can't hurt.

Since you know what excess weight doesn't do for you, why not turn the sock inside out and ask what it could possibly be doing *for* you. (Yes, here I am again, asking this question!) Why might you need to be overweight? What are your real beliefs about weight? And I want you to really listen to the answers. Listen to the *literal* answers.

Are you a heavyweight as a personality or a lightweight? Which would you like to be? Which do you admire? Can a heavyweight be pushed around?

Does having an ample figure show a person is well fed, surrounded by abundance? What do you need to cover up with your fat? Are you hiding some deep feeling of vulnerability or self-hate? Are you starving for love and trying to meet that need with food? After all, your mother first showed her love by feeding her baby. Did she not feed you well enough?

Do you find the world a cold and rejecting place and therefore protect yourself with layers of fat to keep you afraid and insured against the lean years to come? Are you be afraid of physical intimacy? Fat people are not considered to really desirable in our society as skinny people.

Have you or are you needing to pad yourself from the blows of life and rejection? Are fat people really jollier, or are you trying to hide a mean streak you are ashamed of? Are you padding some awful truth?

In other words, what is the real *dis-ease* in your life?

Look, ladies and gents. I am a veteran of the weight-losing wars. I have spent thousands of dollars and as many hours in seven different and costly weight-loss programs and bought an untold numbers of books and do-it-yourself plans. They all worked for a while until eventually and inevitably those old deep-seated beliefs of mine re-emerged from their shallow graves where I tried in vain to bury them. Fat has replaced muscle and discouragement has replaced hope. But I have learned one thing. I've got the answers right inside this little ole plump body, heart and mind of mine.

All those people who tried to help me lose weight didn't have a chance because I didn't examine and change my beliefs about myself and my weight first. Until you do that, everything else you try is a waste of time and money. If you want a helping hand, look at the end of your arm and then place that hand on your heart and head, and ask those really tough questions. You won't be disappointed. You may even be surprised.

§

Food for the Soul

Life is full of anniversary dates that bring back memories, happy and sad, and help us to chronicle our walk through life. Life itself gives us the anniversaries of the seasons, each offering its own unique celebrations through which we feel a rhythm and maybe even a reason existence.

It is probably a little early by the calendar to be heralding spring, but I'm feeling the newness of the season which seems even newer and fresher when it comes early like it is as I write. My dogs are sprawled out in the warming sun unperturbed by the cool breeze that ruffles their still-thick winter coats. They have exhausted themselves playing like the puppies they are not.

I, too, write this while being kissed by precious sun rays and thinking what a good idea early afternoon siestas are. Springtime is the season when a young man's fancy turns to love—and a young woman's and an old woman's and an old man's.

Love is, after all, the food of the soul and can be the difference between life and death even when the body is clean and fed. Year after year, we are confronted daily with the physical starvation of thousands in Africa. Their will to live is obvious as they travel hundreds of miles under unbearable conditions with only the hope of finding food to fuel them. But that is my point. Hope and love for life is the real fuel for the soul that may then drive the body beyond its normal limits.

So what about those who lose the will to live even when well fed? For any student of psychology, the works of John Bowlby on separation and attachment are classics. He studied the orphans of England during WWII and the condition he called *marasmus,* which was a physical emaciation to the point of death, spawned from emotional loneliness and lack of stimulation.

Though the children (mostly infants) were well fed and bathed daily, the staff was so outnumbered that there was no time left for holding, talking to or interacting in any way with each child. As a result, the children simply died of loneliness, of a broken heart if you will.

In other words, man really cannot survive on bread alone, which is why solitary confinement is such a harsh punishment. In today's world, at least in this country, we don't see the dramatic kinds of examples that Bowlby found. Orphanages are by and large a thing of the past, at least in the western world, and thanks to his work and that of others after him, even premature babies in the solitary confinement of their incubators are now rocked, stroked and talked to several times a day.

However, I think we see marasmus by the inches all around us in people whose souls are slowly dying for lack of meaningful interaction with others. The suffering of the North Africans is a poignant reminder of how intense and intimate life can be when we feel and respond to the suffering of others. As the third world nations fight just to survive, they have much to teach those of us in affluent nations.

Our affluence has replaced love. We give things instead of ourselves. We buy objects of intimacy instead of taking time to touch. We read books on touching instead of taking time to talk. We talk to strangers, counselors, instead of to each other. We feed our bodies to excess instead of feeding our souls.

And what is the food of the soul? Why, love, of course. Wherever you can give it is where you will also find it—in the open face of a child; in the begging hand of a street person; in the harried frown of a store clerk; in the worried face of a parent; in the exhausted slump of a teacher; in the tears of a friend; in your own dark hours of loneliness.

In early spring, the sun's rays seem more caressing, more loving than at any other time of year. The warmth after a cold winter promises much and indeed delivers much. As the sun touches the earth, the earth responds with new life. So it is with people when touched by love. When you choose love over hate and fear, you choose life over death.

§